HIGH TIDES

———— & ————

OPEN HANDS

*A GUIDE TO GRIEF
AND LIVING BROKEN-OPEN*

KATHERINE FLYNN PLUCINSKY

PINA PUBLISHING 🍍 SEATTLE

The stories and events that appear in this book are true.

Text copyright © 2021 by Katherine Flynn Plucinsky
Cover design by Katherine Flynn Plucinsky © 2021 by Katherine Flynn Plucinsky
Cover photo by © 2021 by Katherine Flynn Plucinsky
Interior book design by © 2021 by Katherine Flynn Plucinsky

All rights reserved, including the right of reproduction in whole or in part in any form. First edition, 2021.

For information about special discounts for bulk purchases contact: sales@pinapublishing.com

Manufactured in the United States of America
Library of Congress Cataloging-in-Publication Data Plucinsky, Katherine.

Summary:
High Tides & Open Hands is Katherine Flynn Plucinsky's debut novel, a courageous and intimate memoir about her experience surrounding the loss of her "person" and best friend. Through a mixture of poetry and prose, Plucinsky reveals what it is like to be completely consumed by the shifting waves of grief. Her process is put on full display, as is her connection to God, a relationship which she considers foundational. The strength of her faith is tested, but ultimately fortified through the power of surrender. Indeed, this is a story of hope, healing, and resiliency from a young author who provides us with an embodied example of what it means to live a life that is broken, open.

ISBN:
978-1-943493-42-5 (paperback)
978-1-943493-48-7 (ebook)
978-1-943493-43-2 (hardcover)

[1. Memoir-Nonfiction. 2. Poetry. 3. Spiritual-Nonfiction.
4. Self-help-Nonfiction. 5. Transformation. 6. Empowerment.]

This book is dedicated to all of my friends and family who have encouraged me to pursue my writing for years.

To my person, Courteney Saeman.
I hope this book makes you proud from above.
I can feel you in all that I do & all that I am.

To God,
I promised I would share with the world what You have done for me.
I hope these words do justice in honoring You.

And lastly, this book is dedicated to myself.
This process has been my main outlet during a hard time,
and has healed my soul in a thousand ways.
I knew you could do it, you brave soul.

Table of Contents

PART I: DIVE UNDER
- divine pursuit 13
- deeper place 16
- interior life 17

PART II: WAVES OF GRIEF
- grief diaries introduction 21
- dear best friend 25
- grief diaries 27
- relearning to live 39
- open your still-bleeding hands 43
- fingerprints 47
- unconventional grief 49

PART III: IMPACT ZONE
- the in-between 53
- undertow 55
- good father 58
- persevering love 64
- henry brown 65
- coping 68
- look deeper 70

PART IV: SWIM AGAINST THE CURRENT
- take back your power 75
- bravery 78
- twenty-three 81
- codependency 83
- i am water 86

PART V: LET GO

- art of surrendering 91
- empty yourself 95
- childlike 100
- rest 102
- let people be there for you 106
- remain grounded 108
- holy hour 110
- soft days & easy breaths 115

PART VI: STAND & RIDE

- 21 years young 119
- fall in love with being alive 122
- acceptance 127
- home 130

Introduction

Words have always been the way that I have processed the world. This book started out as just that: my own processing.

I've always considered myself a spiritual being - it is the human experience that I have been on a journey of unraveling and learning to live. This is a collection of my human experience, to be raw and real amidst suffering and to remain raw and real in the healing, too. It is a testament in trying to understand the messiness and beauty and adventure that comes with the privilege of being alive. It is my ode to express the necessity for spirituality, and to display the rhythm of God's paint strokes in my own life, that hopefully resonate with discovering His rhythm in yours.

Amidst the waves of life, one of the most powerful forces on Earth, we must learn to open our hands in surrender to God, and to remain open through it all - even in our breaking.

With lower lows comes an ability to experience higher highs, and our bandwidth gets altogether stretched in both directions. Life breaks us in so many ways. Becoming broken can cause us to live from a victim mentality and close ourselves off to the world out of fear, or we can choose differently. We can heal others with our brokenness, by remaining open and inviting people into it. The sooner I accept the crosses that are uniquely and intentionally mine, the sooner my personal crosses become redemptive.

com·pas·sion : to suffer with

I would not take away any of the trials and mountains I've faced because of the unfolding resiliency that has emerged from deep within me. I will make purpose of suffering. I will share it, speak it, write it, if only to touch one other human life for the better; if only to symbolically hold the hand of another individual going through something they don't quite know how they're going to make it through. To be compassionate is to suffer with one another.

I'm here, and I'm reaching for your hand.
I invite you to take it.

My desire would be to have coffee with each person that picks up this book and to be totally present to you; listening to your story, your dreams, your fears, your faith, your grief, what has hurt you, and also what has healed you. Maybe someday we can. But for now, my hope is that you can find pieces of hope, healing, and freedom to hold onto tightly in these pages. May these words allow you to tap into your own resiliency, and may your strength and courage surprise you.

Welcome to being human. It's nice to have you along for the ride.

"You can't control the waves, but you can learn to surf."

– Jon Kabat-Zinn

PART I:
DIVE UNDER

"From birth, man carries the weight of gravity on his shoulders. He is bolted to earth. But man has only to sink beneath the surface and he is free."

– Jacques Yves Cousteau

DIVINE PURSUIT

it's unlike anything i've ever experienced.

all-encompassing
washing over my entire being
like an ocean wave
– gentle but powerful –
crashing over the sand
and taking it back to the vast sea along with it.
the total immersion and complete union.

God's love.

it never *tires* of pursuing us;
and this is what is so radical to me.

i tire.
i tire quickly,
with much concern over the protection of my own heart
that i wouldn't dare put myself out there,
i wouldn't dare keep fighting,
with the possibility of rejection and abandonment.

cory asbury says it beautifully
explaining his song
reckless love:
"God's love is so fearless,
so utterly detached from the consequences
in regards to His safety, comfort, and well-being.
His love isn't guarded.
it isn't selfish or self-serving,
it isn't sly,
it's actually quite
c h i l d - l i k e.
God doesn't wonder what He'll attain or lose by putting Himself on the line.
He simply puts Himself out there on the slim chance
that you and i might just glance His way and give Him that love in return.
this might seem like a ridiculous concept to us
that God gives His heart so completely and outrageously
that if rejected, we would think it irreversibly broken.
yet He gives himself away
again, and again, and again."

so all of the things you deem yourself unworthy of love for,
the insecurities you don't let anyone close enough to see,
the weight of what you consider to be your brokenness,
– the "burdens" and "roadblocks" you place before you –
s h a t t e r
with a single glance
when the Father looks at you.

*your stubbornness is insignificant
to the power of His pursuit of you.*

*your defense mechanisms don't even touch
the magnitude of His desire for you.*

compared to His ache for you
these things are light
and easy
and joyful
and only add to the captivation
that God has for who you are.

no matter how many times we push away,
no matter how many times we choose something else,
the pursuit is so steady
so consistent
so unconditional + unchanging,
completely covered in fidelity.

God continues to be devoted to us
in all of our wanderings,
even when we are not devoted back.
God believes in us
when we fail to believe in Him
because this love
does not seek anything in return.

how can *we* love
with a love that persists
despite the cost?

we grow weary
of fighting for one another,
of walking beside each other.
we grow tired
of what love demands,
of the sacrifices to be made

and the emptying of ourselves
to make more space,
more capacity
for the other.

but at the end of our lives
are we really going to be glad that we stayed back
– reserved and protected –
from that possible heart break?
that potential friendship?
that hand we should have reached out,
but didn't?

or are we going to wish that we loved
a little more *deeply*,
a little more *fully*,
a little more *Godly*?

the people who live with a love
that is loyal + unrelenting + selfless:
thank you for bringing God to me
in incredibly tangible ways.
that your very hands and hearts
become
the hands and hearts of God touching me.

remember you are not a burden.
you are a joy,
a delight,
a gift.
& hear me when I say:

the Heavenly King,
the Divine Author,
your Higher Power,
Our Creator,
will choose you
every // single // time.

you are worthy of the fight.
you are worthy of the pursuit.
  again,
    and again,
      and *a g a i n*.

DEEPER PLACE

i'm learning to live out of that deeper place
beyond the fear response,
beyond the self-reliance,
beyond the planning, controlling, and grasping.

the deeper place
where i'll be taken care of.
where i choose
Your presence over my problems,
surrender over solutions,
trust over certainty,
and faith over a fickle + false security in things of this world.

i'm learning to release
into the deeper part of my heart
for there You are.
and where You are,
i desire to be.

clinging to control and solutions,
has only stolen my peace.
You are peace.
You are not a spirit of rushing, hurrying,
indecision, or unrest.
i can rest in Your trust
because there will always be
one more thing to do.
peace simply comes from spending time with You.
so let me be spirit-led,
following your guidance
with every single step.

i'm looking for the answers
God,
but You are the Answer.

THE INTERIOR LIFE

exchange your gold + silver.
the richest gift this life has to offer
is the interior life.

stay rooted in
divine intimacy.
always.

underneath the chaos of the exterior world,
past the years of built-up defense mechanisms,
exists the interior life.
the light that dwells within.
beyond the waves that crash around me,
beyond the storms that strike above me,
beyond the fighting that surrounds me,
and the circumstances that i have no control over,
beyond it all –
lies an entire
sacred
world.

as the waves get closer
and fear paralyzes me,
God grabs my hand
and pulls me under.

i dive
under the chaos
into the calm break.
of spirituality
and soul.

a quiet stillness
of rest and restoration.
receiving, learning, loving.
i watch transformation
unravel like a red carpet
slowly unfolding before me.
and something is deeply peaceful about the quiet stirrings taking place.
there's no need to prove anything here,

no need to post about it
because this is sacred space for only me and you, Lord.
it's a deeply intimate place where i am
grounded, rooted, and brought back to the Truth.

it is where i'm reminded that i belong
to my Creator.
and that i have access to Him at all times.

even if everything in this world was stripped from me;
all my belongings,
everything that I call my "own,"
was stolen –
i would *still* have this one thing.

it is in the deepest recesses of my heart
where peace abides,
where God abides.
here, i find a breathtaking silence
and God speaks to me
gently + softly.

it is an expansive opening
and it exceeds all of my expectations of
who and what God is.

remember, you have this place, too.

when the waves grow bigger,
will you take God's hand
and dive under
to explore your own interior life?
to silence all the noise,
all the voices that surround you
from society + culture,
from people,
and perhaps even from your own ego.
to hear the quiet arising of Truth
and to feel a peace that is unlike anything this world can offer,
unrelated to your exterior circumstances.

you owe it to yourself
to find out what it's all about
and what you will discover is
richer
than you can imagine.

PART II:
WAVES OF GRIEF

"Grief is like the ocean. It comes in waves, ebbing and flowing.
Sometimes the water is calm, sometimes it is overwhelming.
All we can do is learn to swim."

– Vicki Harrison

*** These are my grief diaries.

I can see the different and specific stages of grief so clearly etched into these words –even when in the moment I didn't know where I was. I'm grateful I wrote through the process as it was happening because I'm now able to look back at my journey. I can see the exact things that hardened me, the things that softened me, and the things that healed me. I can see the natural process of grief, the way my mind and body felt, thought, and expressed everything they had to in order to get me to this point. The denial was just as important as the anger, as the bargaining was to the depression. Acceptance comes in moments and days, but I know there is so much more still to come.

I encourage you to document your own processing so you can hold close your unique grief journey. It is yours, and yours alone.
Remember, you are exactly where you need to be.
And I personally want to say, I'm sorry you are going through this. It's not fair.***

(For anyone in the grief process now or anyone trying to understand the grief process because someone you know is going through it, here are my raw thoughts and feelings from the trenches of grief.
The pain is unbearable, but it helps to know someone understands.
And <u>actually</u> understands.)

"i'm so sorry."
"call me as soon as you get this."
"please answer."
"i can't believe it."
"are you okay?"

i woke up
february 2nd, 2017
to dozens of texts like this
from people i hadn't spoken to in years,
from family,
from friends,
having no idea what any of it meant.

my heart started beating out of my chest
as i scrolled through the messages and missed calls.
something isn't right, i thought.
something happened.
someone died.
i didn't hear from courteney.
she would have been the first person to call me.
something happened to courteney.

Let me rewind. I met a girl freshman year of high school. She was really tall, pretty awkward, very sweet, and mildly sarcastic. Her name was Courteney Saeman. Not knowing anyone else in Photoshop 101, we sat next to each other in class. One day, I had taken off my shoes under the desk and Courteney said with a disgusted look on her face, "It smells like feet in here." Although I nodded in agreement, under my breath I started laughing and quickly put my shoes back on. Pretty soon, we became inseparable.

We started having weekly school night sleepovers. It would be 10 p.m., and just as Courteney began to fall asleep, I would wake her up by jumping on the bed. I wasn't tired yet, so *she* wasn't allowed to be tired yet. "Don't go to sleep! I'm bored. Let's do something. What do you want to do?" I would yell as I was jumping up and down on the bed, back and forth, over her. My other friends would probably push me off or yell at me about having to wake up early, but Courteney just laughed. This girl was 6 foot. I'm 5'6. She's about half a foot taller than me and could have easily gotten me to stop. But she could never be mad about my shenanigans, no matter how annoying they were. Her response was always laughter. Even when she tried to tell me to stop with a serious face, she would break out mid-sentence, giggling. Her solution was to grab the comforter, drag it into her walk-in closet, and lock the door so she could sleep in peace. But she would always manage to get her revenge at 6 a.m. the next morning by not letting me sleep. This was the routine for our school night sleepovers, every week. Somehow it never got old.

> Courteney was all things to me. That is why her love felt so similar to the love of God.
> The way God molds to what we need in each moment – Courteney was somehow able to do the same.
> "What do you want for dinner?" she asked me like a mother, on days when I needed a little extra nurturing.
> "You're so much better than that," she would confront me like a father, on days when I needed to be called out.
> "Did you take my shirt?" she yelled at me like a sister, on days when I just needed a shirt.
> "I don't know how you do it, but on your hardest days, you shine the brightest," she comforted me like a therapist, on days when I couldn't see my own strength.

Courteney was always full of surprises. Going to colleges in different states allowed for a lot of room to surprise each other. Somehow, living far apart made us closer than ever.

For my 21st birthday, I was dancing with my roommate in the living room at a party. I suddenly saw *Courteney* walk through the door, her radiant smile beaming off her face. (Mind you - I went to college on the *other* side of the country from her.) After a few minutes of my own shock, a few tears, and then squeezing her until she couldn't breathe, she asked me to come outside to get something, and there, my two other friends from high school were standing. They all flew out to Cincinnati to surprise me for my birthday, and somehow managed to keep the whole thing a secret. I felt more love that weekend than I had ever experienced before in my life, as my two worlds collided with all of the people I loved in one place.

Another time, I was coming home from college for Christmas break and we hadn't seen each other in 6 months. That may not be a long time, but for us, it felt like an entire *decade*. She texted me as I was boarding my flight, "I'm really sorry, but I have a test I didn't know about. I won't be able to come pick you up from the airport. This week is pretty crazy, but I can try to come see you when things get less busy." I was bummed and made other arrangements.

When I landed in Denver, I took the train to Baggage Claim, and as I went up the escalator;

classic,

I see Courteney standing there, per usual, waiting for me with a giant smile and her sneaky surprises.

So now, as I fly back home to Denver, I take the train to Baggage Claim, go up the escalator, put my headphones in, and keep my head *down*. It just hurts too much. Too many times, have I searched for her face among the strangers waiting with signs and flowers. And every single time, no matter how long it's been, I'll convince myself this whole thing was a terrible dream. It was a joke she was playing on me, all so she could surprise me at the airport at this moment. My eyes search and search, until I finally remember again why I won't see her face in the crowd.

I go through this ritual every time I travel. So I've learned to cut my thoughts off before I even begin the search. *Just put your head down. Don't look at the crowd. She's not going to be there.*

DEAR BEST FRIEND

(1 week)

Hi Biggie.

I've been putting this off because it would mean that this is real.
The best thing in my life was taken from me in a single
i n s t a n t.
They say true love is putting someone else's happiness above your own,
and although I am in excruciating pain, as it feels like you took a big piece of me when you left,
I know from glimpses when I've experienced God that you are in nothing but complete peace and incomprehensible joy.

A week ago, you said you felt closer to God than you ever have, but you had no idea how much closer you were going to get.
We had so many plans... we were going to live together after graduation, move to California, you were supposed to be my maid of honor, but I guess God's plans were bigger than ours.

I found a scrapbook you gave me before we went to college and in it you said, "I hope you know that you are hands down going to be my hardest goodbye, but no matter what happens or where life takes us next, you will always be my best friend." We never were good at goodbyes, so instead we would say "see you soon."
Court, you will never stop being my best friend. No amount of time or distance will change that to make it past tense. You used to get jealous when I'd make new friends, but I told you I'd never replace you and I haven't. I never can, because finding someone like you is rare; truth be told I'll never find someone like you again.
Someone who brought 3 laundry baskets into my house and stayed for a week without even asking.
Someone so goofy, who made everyone laugh with your awkward dance moves.
Someone who never gave up on people because you always saw the good in them.
Someone who was so humble, so breathtakingly beautiful with those green eyes, and had absolutely no idea because you never took yourself or life too seriously.
You've taught me so much.
You were always determined to be a good person, no matter what. You didn't believe anything was an excuse to not be a good person.
You were fearless. You were the most selfless and genuine person I knew, so happy to go above and beyond for others.

KATHERINE FLYNN PLUCINSKY

You kept me grounded with your loving honesty, never afraid to call me higher. I could get through anything because I knew I'd have you by my side. You did everything for me.

21 years is too soon.

I don't want to see a world without you in it, but I've already felt so many moments, like laying in your bed or being with your family, where I feel so much strength and peace that could only be coming from you.

Some of the hardest days of my life are yet to come, but I know you'd want me to be laughing and celebrating your life and our friendship. You were the best possible person to "do life" with, and for that I'm forever grateful. I have no regrets with you because you knew that I've never been closer or loved anyone more than you.

You said that you needed to get home before dark, and my sweet NeyNey, you did. Welcome home.

I can't wait to jump on you again, even though you're a foot taller than me, and for all the therapeutic drives we will have in Heaven, singing at the top of our lungs, for sleepover after sleepover, for the endless supply of chai tea and salty foods.

Not goodbye, but see you soon. And don't worry, I'll still call you for everything. Hope the reception is okay up there.

I love you eternally
my best friend and other half,

Your Flynn (Smalls)

(2 weeks)

I barely had the strength to get on the airplane by myself to fly home for the funeral. Crying publicly had quickly become something I couldn't care less about. Other people's opinions became completely irrelevant after my world was flipped upside down. Through checking on my bags, security, the endless lines, and the entire 3 and a half hours of the flight, I sobbed. I looked out at the clouds, thinking, "Are you up here?"

It was the night of the open casket and we were gathering at the church to say a rosary for Courteney's soul. I was terrified of the moments to follow. My closest friends from high school met me at the back of the church when I got there so we could walk up together. They had already seen her in the casket, but they wanted to be with me for that moment, and I was incredibly thankful, because I couldn't have done it alone.

A moment no one should have to experience.

People came up to me as we waited in line, and I stood there lifelessly receiving hugs. People who barely knew her were sobbing in my arms as they tried comforting me. I stood there completely empty and stiff. I became angry because it was only making it more real. *Stop hugging me. Stop crying. Stop apologizing. Nothing's wrong. Nothing happened. Stop making it real.*

I walked up with fear and dread, but also emotions of longing and exhilaration – because all I wanted was to be close to my person. Every ounce of my being was craving Courteney's presence. Whatever that looked like. I didn't care. I just needed her. I wanted *her* to be the one to make everything better and the one to comfort me through this. I thought with each step in line, that maybe I would finally feel the way her comfort had solved any problem I had gone through before. After she died, out of habit I called and texted her endlessly. I kept forgetting why she couldn't get me through this one. The truth began to sink in with every voicemail and unanswered text.

I arrived at the front of the church, holding hands with my friends, and found myself completely numb. I stared for minutes, waiting and watching in hope for her chest to move up and down.

But nothing.

I couldn't comprehend it. Here was her body. Her hands were recognizable, with her bitten-down fingernails.

But everything else wasn't. "You're not here," I thought, "this isn't you." The light and radiance was gone, although her body appeared the same. The essence of her soul was not here, in her body, in this casket. This moment really confirmed it for me. Who we are is in our *s o u l s*. *That* is our being. Not this earthly shell.

My mom walked up as I stood there, unable to stop staring, and she grabbed my hand. "Our girl," she whispered, through tears. Next, she fearlessly grabbed Courteney's hand and kissed her forehead. "There was no one better," she said. I wanted to do the same, but I was scared. I didn't want anything to change the way I thought about her, the way I would remember her. I slowly reached my hand out to touch her cold hands and kissed her cold forehead.

She was not here.

I pulled a note out of my jacket that I had written to her and tucked it into her casket. Then I pulled out two necklaces from my pocket. One had the word "Biggie" engraved on it, and the other one had the word "Smalls." I held both of the necklaces in my right palm, thinking *this is the last time these necklaces will be in the same place. This is the last time Courteney and I will be in the same place, at least physically.* I moved her hair to the side and put the Biggie necklace around her neck, fastening the clasp. And then I fastened the Smalls necklace around mine. "We will always be connected," I prayed to her.

Perhaps I imagined,
but perhaps I knew,
that she was watching it all.
Not from her casket –
but maybe next to me,
maybe from above me.
Maybe she was still here –
somehow.

The next day was her funeral.

We knew our Court would want us to spice things up and shy away from the all-black, depressing funeral thing. Her step-mom, sisters, cousins, closest friends, and I all wore dresses, jean jackets, and cowboy boots. During the procession at the beginning, the casket came first, and then we all followed down the aisle behind her, one at a time. I couldn't help but think that this is what should be happening on her *wedding day*, not her funeral.

The man who gave the eulogy used my words. He read out loud what I sent to him when he asked why Courteney was so special to the people that loved her. As we went up for Communion, the casket was at the front of the church in the middle of the aisle by the priest. I gently grazed my hand along her casket and kissed it, right before receiving Communion. It was like I was walking up to Jesus and her standing there together, as I received the Bread of Life with a firm, "Amen." Amen in Hebrew means "so be it." This was a bold proclamation I was making, whether I realized it at the time or not.

There was that feeling again –she's still here somehow.

At the reception, people continued giving me their condolences and hugs, but I don't fully remember much. One friend later told me that she had never seen somebody so much not present in their body, as when she saw me that day. Courteney's four closest friends and I went up to speak in front of everyone together. Once again, I thought, this should be happening at her *wedding*, not her funeral.

I don't think anyone got through their speech - family included- without breaking down. This just wasn't how it was supposed to be. How do you even find the words to explain what a person meant to you? There really aren't any. Not logically, anyway. Not in the English dictionary.

We headed to the cemetery.

This was the place it all became real to me. The most gut-wrenching, **powerless** part. Watching this machine slowly lower my favorite person in the world into the ground. I went outside of my body. The other things I could handle– but not this.

Although physically I remained still and silent, in my head I was screaming at the top of my lungs, "No, no, no," over and over again, louder and louder, falling on the wet grass; but only in my head. Physically –I appeared still, motionless, blank. Inside, I was crumbling. Courteney's dad came over to hug me and I collapsed into his arms. This time, not in my head. My body buckled. This poor man just lost his little girl, his own *child*, and here he was – comforting me, holding me up. No parent should ever have to go through their child's death before their own. That is truly hell on earth.

After the service, everyone slowly trickled out of the cemetery, one by one, driving away. I sat on the grass next to where she was just buried. I heard my mom's voice in the background say to my friends, "I can't get her to leave."

"Katherine," they said, after walking over, sitting beside me, and putting their arms around me. "I can't leave her. I can't. We promised not to leave each other, no matter what," I testified. We were the last ones there.

Helping me rise from the ground, they carried me, one on each side. I could barely stand, I was crying so hard.

As we walked away, three girls in cowboy boots and jean jackets, with tears that would stain our faces for months. We knew things would never be the same again. We knew this wasn't what 21 was supposed to be like.

That night, I drove up to Red Rocks. That had always been my place of escape. Something about the mountains and overlook of Denver could clear my head instantly. I was with someone very dear to me. He and Courteney were my two biggest sources of stability through the worst of times. Together, they would talk about doing anything to protect me and to see me happy. I will never be able to find words of gratitude about two people who sacrificed more for me. Two people who always made me feel incredibly safe, no matter what was going on in the world.

As we looked up into the night sky, trying to even comprehend the day we just had, there was the most vibrant rainbow in the shape of a circle around the entire full moon. To this day, it was one of the most wild and beautiful things I've ever seen. Peace washed over my being.

She's watching over me.

(1 month)

I went back to Cincinnati after the funeral to finish my senior year of college. Only one of my professors asked how I was doing after I returned from the funeral.

Although I attended classes, I don't remember anything I learned the remainder of my senior year. Nothing felt like it mattered anymore. Learning how to market a product felt so irrelevant. I was numb to it all. Yet, at the same time, I felt everything so deeply. It was an experience of paradoxes. I would roll my eyes at the things my peers complained about, and I felt both envy and pity for a world in which insignificant things are made to be so big.

I physically showed up to class so I wouldn't get points deducted, but I couldn't help but get sucked into the whirlwind of my thoughts, playing the denial game for the entirety of the ninety-minute class. A continual mental and emotional fight that was silently fought and unseen.

The most painful part was the *denial*. When I would wake up, I would think everything was fine for just a moment - and **that** was the worst part. The denial meant I had to live through the realization of reality a thousand times throughout the day. Acting like nothing happened would mean that sooner or later, I would have to remember and come to terms with it all over again. It was like every day I was reliving the exact moment I got the phone call with the news. This happened for what seemed like every five minutes. A single day felt like an eternity. Maybe that's what it feels like when people say God lives outside of time.

I would sleep just to escape this ongoing realization. And then I would dread waking up and thinking life was normal, because moments later every single emotion would hit me harder than ever. I just wanted to be able to grasp it, so this cycle would end. It was emotionally deteriorating me.

The day after the accident when everyone was posting on Facebook, I couldn't even look. I didn't want it to be true. Anger filled me as I threw my phone. "*Stop making it real,*" I thought. As if people posting or not posting a picture of Courteney determined if she had actually died. But any ounce of control I had, I clung to. If I didn't see it, maybe it wasn't real. I didn't check Facebook for weeks.

I remember one specific and random day, about a month in, when I woke up and I didn't have to play the back and forth denial game. My thoughts weren't fighting each other like they usually did. I woke up with awareness that she had died. And on that day things got better, because that morning, I woke up not in denial. And the next morning. And the next.

From that one random morning, it became slightly less painful to manage because I could accept reality and figure out how to cope with it, instead of having to fight it over and over again. Instead of having to *live* it over and over again. From getting the bad news, questioning everything, being overcome with despair and doubt, and confronting the truth — denial was exhausting.

The process of denial was more painful than actually living in the hard truth.

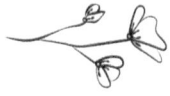

(5 months)

Writing has always been an outlet of mine. I love words. But for the first time in my life, I have felt a pain so great that no words can manage to explain it righteously.

Grief (n.) synonyms:
pain. sorrow. misery. sadness. anguish. heartache. agony. suffering. desolation.

This whole grief thing has been a messy process. It doesn't go from one stage to the next like they say - cut and clear - until finally you happily accept the death of your loved one and continue living your life like before. One moment I'll be angry and sad, the next I'll somehow feel peace that Courteney is in a better place, and then the next, I'll be right back to step one, denying the reality of the loss of my best friend.

Pretty much most days consist of me thinking how I would do anything to have her back on Earth with me. I find myself bargaining with God to give her back to me. I try to make deals in prayer, saying I'll never do something again if you bring her back. I have dreams all the time that she never died. In them, she always just laughs and says the whole thing was a joke. Crazy thought processes can happen when the human mind attempts to grasp death. There aren't many things in life that feel this permanent.

With all of these emotions and thoughts taking place internally, the fast-paced world we live in is no longer something I can keep up with. What blows my mind is how I never once questioned the fast-paced way of life until now. It's just what you do. You move on. You have your two-week time frame *(if that)* to grieve and then – time's up. Back to work, back to life. You have to because everyone else is still living their lives the same as before, like *n o t h i n g* has happened. We live in a world where after a few months of the most life-shattering tragedy you've ever experienced, you need to be okay, and not only okay, but thriving.

I should be fine by now, right?

People stop asking how you are, assuming that because you've smiled, the gut-wrenching hole in your stomach is gone. You can feel the "tiring out" of your social media posts expressing how much you miss the person who died.
As the days pass, people start responding with, "it's been a while since it happened," like a time-frame really determines what you're experiencing, when it is allowed to be hard, and when your time of sadness is overdue. As if your grief has an expiration date, like food at the grocery store.

I've learned how rare it is to find people that are supportive for the entirety of the time you are going through grief because of how long of a process it is, and how it doesn't allow for the fast-paced conclusions that we are used to. *Patience is required when loving someone through grief.*

Mostly it's just because people don't understand it until they've been through it. There is no ill intent. In fact, most people don't even realize they aren't being there in ways that they could be. Other people's pain just makes us uncomfortable. To see someone we love in pain causes an emotional reaction in us, and so we want to do something to stop it as quickly as possible. We don't know how to deal with our own reaction to another's pain, so we try to avoid it altogether. We can't make it better or fix it, and that is too hard to deal with. We will do anything to shy away from talking about death until it slaps us in the face and we are forced to deal with it.

I, myself, was a victim of this, until the night of February 1st, 2017 – the night of a deadly car accident that changed my life forever. Courteney was driving home and her wheels hit black ice. She spun out into the opposite lane and collided with another driver.

*And just like that,
she was gone.*

This was something no one could see coming. People drive under the influence all of the time, and nothing happens. But here was a girl driving home from work, doing nothing wrong, and yet she was in the hands of something beyond her control. Mother Nature was more powerful than her that night.

Truth be told, I had no idea what to say or do when someone I knew lost someone they loved. People in my life have died before, but until Courteney died (until my most constant person died) I didn't understand it really. I didn't know how to help ease the pain people were experiencing. It truly is a helpless feeling.

These are a few things I wish I knew before:

The pain doesn't lessen over time, people just learn to find a way to live with it.

Ask how they are, even if it's uncomfortable.

Keep checking up on someone, no matter how much time has passed.

Talk about the person who died. Just because they died, doesn't mean their legacy should. The person is thinking about their loved one a majority of the time anyway, so you're not making them sad by bringing it up.

Be patient with the random breakdowns.

Don't act surprised if as time passes they still get extremely sad. Their sadness is going to be caused by this tragedy for a long, long time, and that's okay.

Don't rush anyone to "move on" or come out of denial. That period of grace is so necessary for the healing process.

Time is truly irrelevant when it comes to grief "check points."

Don't take it personally if they don't initiate conversation as often as they used to. They have a lot less energy than normal.

Avoid clichés if possible. Yes, we know they're in a better place. No, it does not make it hurt less.

Not only did someone they love die, but they also lost a part of themselves in the process. Don't expect them to be as energetic and happy as they were because sometimes they just aren't feeling like themselves.

It's okay to sit with them and let them be sad. You don't have to try to make them happy or fix things.
Sometimes it just sucks, and that's okay. "I'm sorry," or "I can't imagine," goes a lot farther than trying to be overly optimistic.

They are now constantly consumed by a fear of losing people closest to them. You are probably one of those people.

Even if someone has never had anxiety or depression, they can start to as a result of the death of a loved one.

Presence does a lot more than words can to comfort someone.

If you're personally going through this, please be patient with yourself. You deserve all the time in the world to be sad about it and heal from this the way you want. Feel what you need to. I also urge you to keep talking to God even if you're angry, and be honest. Yelling at God is better than not talking to Him.

Grief can be your worst enemy, but also your greatest teacher. Continue to learn from the process.

(11 months)

This year is going to be my launching year – or so I like to call it. As the new year is approaching, I'm hoping *(just hoping)* that my suffering is going to launch me into something far beyond what I could've ever imagined.

It's safe to say this has been the worst and hardest year of my entire life. Pretty much everything in my life looks different from this time last year. Some components of the year included death, loneliness, loss of friendships, change, desolation, and grappling with a lack of control. I have experienced suffering in the most raw and real way. How is it that I've looked at the cross a thousand times, but never understood what an unjust and unfair world we lived in until the passing of my best friend?

My biggest fear became a reality. The person that was part of me, and I, a part of her, was abruptly taken right from my hands. I'm not sure if we were more like sisters or an old married couple.

Her family was mine, and my family was hers.
(a gift I feel especially grateful for now)

Her calming and playful presence made everything okay, which is why her absence is so incredibly loud. On some days, all I can do is scream to the point that nothing comes out.

If I can make it through this, then nothing in this world can touch me. There is such a sense of *fearlessness* in that which is bolstered by the fact that I now have a fearless, 6'0 (sorry Court, I mean 5'12) guardian angel who has my back at all times. She always took care of me on Earth, but I feel the vastness and intensity of her protection even more now. It's a powerful feeling. No one was more protective over me than she was.

After my world was shattered, I had to learn to relive life in many ways, because nothing from that point on would ever be the same. It's like losing a limb. You learn how to survive without that part of yourself, but your life is drastically changed forever. You have to completely rebuild; your sense of everything shifts. That limb will always be gone. She will always be gone.

In the process of relearning, I have come to see the value in little victories. If you have four days of not leaving the house, count the three days that you did. Did you wake up early and get coffee? Did you shower? Did you pray? Did you see the sunset? Did you have a meaningful conversation? Be proud of yourself for those little things and celebrate your victories, no matter how small they may seem.

For me, every day is a different battle. On some days, I feel a renewed sense of energy that I can use to ride whatever wave of self-improvement I envision for myself that day. And other days, I can't get out of bed. *And that's okay.* That's balance. That's healing. That's progress.

I've come face-to-face with human resilience. Even when we don't want to, we keep going. We survive – it's what we do. It's amazing. It's in our biology. Human beings have far more strength within us than we can even begin to grasp. We are capable of immensely more than what we think. If you were to tell me what I would face in this life, that I would experience this level of grief at this young of an age, I would say there's no chance I could make it through that: but here I am doing it. I may be tired and weak and not sure how I'm doing it, but I'm still doing it.

I know my strength and resilience couldn't be coming from anything other than the grace of God and my best friend. Mostly I am okay because of the hope of Heaven and knowing who my God is – that is what really carries me through this: *eternal perspective.*

There are days when I become incredibly angry at God for taking away my closest person, but at the same time, my faith has grown because of how powerfully I can feel

Courteney's presence – as if she's sitting right next to me. Ask the people closest to her and they'll tell you how she has individually and uniquely shown them that she is okay. From their testimonies and the things I've experienced personally, I know this to be true and am continually in awe. This has given me confidence in the reality of God and Heaven.

Every week my roommate, Lindsay, would take this 13-year-old boy with autism to Sunday school. His name was Bryson. She would briefly ask him, "Can we pray for my friend Katherine? She's having a hard time." So they would pray for me together. One day, Bryson's mom texted Lindsay, saying, "Hey, you have a roommate named Katherine, right? I was wondering who Courteney is, and if she's okay?" Lindsay responded, "Courteney is Katherine's best friend who just passed away in a car accident. Why?" Bryson's mom replied, "Wow. I'm speechless. Every Sunday after church, Bryson has been coming home and sitting outside looking up at the sky saying, "Katherine, Court is okay. Court is okay."

Lindsay never mentioned anything about why I was having a hard time, Courteney's name, or that she passed away in a car accident.

Knowing that there has to be something more is what carries me through my earthly suffering. It's a temporary experience. We judge it as good or bad, but in the end it's really all just temporary. Even if I live a hundred wonderful years on this vast and beautiful Earth, knowing I get to spend eternity with Courteney in paradise makes everything okay, especially when the pain feels unbearable. I've gotten a glimpse of how much deeper love will be in Heaven – a love unlike any Earthly love, where you come to rely not on the physical affirmations of tangible love, but rather to be confident in a love that you can no longer see, hear, or touch, but only feel - and feel with *every* ounce of your being. Not even death can separate the intertwining of mine and Courteney's souls… a love like that is awaiting all of us.

Grief has also taught me that less is more when it comes to relationships. Starting my senior year of college, I would have told you that I had a multitude of people that I could rely on for anything. But come May, there were only a few that stuck by me through all of the ups and downs that grief held for me.

& I want to thank those people: To those family members + friends, my heart is exploding with gratitude and I want to thank you from the bottom of my heart. I honestly wouldn't be where I am if it weren't for you picking me up on my bad days and making me laugh, for holding me and letting me cry without judgment, for pushing me to get out of bed and get that coffee, all the while respecting the space and time I needed to heal, while constantly checking to make sure I was okay.

The remainder of my senior year, I couldn't sleep alone. Nights were the worst. I couldn't fall asleep or turn my thoughts off. Anxiety raged as soon as I crawled into bed because the distractions from the day were gone. I needed distractions, as many as possible. I would try to sleep by myself, but when my efforts failed pretty continuously, my roommate would come sleep with me. I truly don't know how I would have survived to graduation without her. She gave me hope in the human capacity to be present to another's suffering, even without fully understanding it yourself. Although she did not experience the death of her best friend so young, she did everything she could to **try** to understand. That meant more than anything.

Lindsay googled, "How to be there for your best friend who lost their best friend." She read articles on grief. She asked questions. She made efforts to understand, so I didn't feel so alone in what I was experiencing. She knelt down into my brokenness and she loved me there, as I was. Not expecting me to rise to meet her on her level and not caring how uncomfortable it was for her, because her only concern was that I wasn't in the pain alone.

So if right now, you are struggling with something and you feel too heavy for someone in your life, just know that those aren't your people. Your people will take your heaviness, get beside you to help you carry it, and love the absolute hell out of you along the way.
You are allowed to feel all that you do and you are allowed to be all that you are. I promise, you are not weak just because your heart feels heavy.
You are not too heavy just because people don't know how to be there for you.

I do believe God wants us to use our brokenness in very real ways. I always have. My belief is that everything we experience has a purpose to make us more compassionate towards others going through something similar. We learn how to be present to another's suffering. We learn how to love better.

The problem with grief is that you can't speed it up, you can't ignore it (not for long anyways). Rather, all you can do is sit with it and *feel* it. So intensely feel it. It's the most fierce and stinging feeling I've ever experienced, a debilitating emotional wave that I never even knew existed. And then when it gets too much, you compartmentalize it and set it aside until it comes back again, without permission. Grief doesn't care where you are, if you're in the middle of something important, it will come and make its home in the pit of your stomach or in the weight of your chest, without even a sign of its arrival.

So no, I will not go through all of that for nothing – I will not sit back and let this year trample me for no absolute reason at all. I will speak it. I will write it. I will make purpose out of it.

Last New Years, over the sound of loud music and our clinking champagne glasses, I looked at Courteney with a smile on my face and said, "Thank God this year is over." Now, what I would give to have that year back. To have that moment in time back; to have one more sleepover, one more forehead kiss, one more road trip singing "It's a Great Day to be Alive" at the top of our lungs, one more awkward dance party, and one more New Years Eve cheers with my favorite person in the world.

Truly appreciate what you have right now because one day you're going to want it all back. May your New Years be full of blessings and may you allow this year to launch you into something great for what's coming next.

RELEARNING TO LIVE

(1 year and 5 months)

My anxiety has been at an all-time high. I've felt really lost with no sense of direction. I needed some time in a beautiful place to clear my head. My body was craving the ocean and my soul was yearning for a place to do some inner work. California was calling my name.

I showed up in Orange County in January with a suitcase so heavy I couldn't even carry it. But by March, I was leaving to go back home with a much lighter load. I spent the time in between unpacking little by little, leaving the things I no longer needed to carry, the things that no longer served me. I had more wounds than I even realized, and I began to let down my walls so God could start to heal each one with His gentle touch.

I think our inadequacy serves a purpose because it makes us totally dependent on God. When we know the limits of our own strength, there is so much power and freedom that comes from walking with God. I look at the story of the disciples coming to Jesus with nothing but five pieces of bread. Jesus took those loaves and multiplied them to feed five hundred people *with* leftovers. When we come with nothing but ourselves, Jesus says it is enough, and multiplies the blessings abundantly. I experienced this firsthand by bringing myself to Him and receiving abundant peace in return.

In California, I relearned how to truly live in the moment. Time had been ticking so slowly the past year. But each and every day, I started by watching the sunrise and ended by watching the sunset. That changed the way I was living because I couldn't wait to wake up and do it again and sit in those moments for as long as I could. I turned off my phone and disconnected from everyone and everything for a month so that I could better connect with myself and God. It helped me to be truly present because I wasn't distracted by anything else and had no choice but to focus on what was right in front of me.

One day, while on a run, I imagined myself at the top of a glass skyscraper and below me, much smaller, were all the people who had hurt me. They could no longer touch me because of the see-through barrier that separated us. The glass was the separation between the past and the present. How can someone touch you if they're not in the same place as you?

In order to be present, I heard someone say they look down at their feet. I've been doing this often in order to stay in the moment. Living in the past has only brought resentment, and living in the future has only brought fear. But when I look down at my feet, there is neither fear nor resentment, just heels or boots.

As difficult as it was not being able to grieve together with her friends and family, I wanted to be at the beach for the one-year anniversary of Courteney's accident. Like any anniversary or birthday related to her, this was a day I was really nervous for. On the afternoon of February 1st, fog enveloped the air from left to right. I wrote "I love you Court" in the sand and watched as the water rolled over my message and pulled it right into the sea. Perhaps all the way to Courteney herself.

The ocean has been my favorite teacher. Sitting in the sand and watching the tides remind me of the waves of grief. Some are big, some are small, some are expected, some you don't notice, and others you don't see coming until they knock you down and hold you under water for what feels like a lifetime.

As I watched the tide dance back and forth, I kept thinking about the question that had consumed me the past year. Who am I without Courteney? I really struggled with my identity after losing her because she was so much a part of me. I didn't know how to live without her. I didn't know who to be without her. She made me the most "me" I've ever felt.

Instead of dwelling on the idea that she took a large part of me with her, I decided that I had to start living enough for the both of us. One of the things she said she loved about me was that I was unapologetically myself, and it was time I found that within me again, even if I didn't know what that would look like without her.

I tend to hold onto the pain because it's one of the only tangible things I have left of her on Earth. People have continuously told me I need to let that pain go and move on, but I've stopped listening. Quite frankly, I have the rest of my life to have a relationship with grief. The journey is mine alone, and I get to define what it is going to look like for myself. We have been taught to use intellect for emotional wounds, but that just doesn't work. Instead, I learned to use peace as a guide. When I feel peace, I know I'm moving in the right direction. No one can tell me what that looks like and what I should or shouldn't do, because each relationship with her was different. Grief is the normal and natural response to loss. But all loss is deeply personal and relational, so every person's journey looks different even if they are grieving the same person. Although I came to California to mend the Courteney-shaped hole in my heart, rediscovering myself is what has been the big takeaway (& there's not a doubt in my mind that she played a huge role in the rediscovery).

I learned to trust myself more and stop seeking validation from other people. When I'm living authentically, the right people are naturally drawn to me. I don't have energy to respond to negative people. Honestly, I barely have energy for anything anymore. When my life is aligned with my values, I am confident in the truth I am living out. I care less about what other people think of me and more about what I think of myself. At 22 years old, I'm just now understanding that I get to decide where to place my energy. That's liberating. I want the people in my life, those who matter, to see a resilient, beautiful, and inspiring person. I want them to see strength and faith and an authentic heart. I've become okay with the fact that not everyone will see those things in me, because the people who are most important will. They are the ones who love me for me.

I also learned that strangers can love you very well in your pain. I went camping in the California desert with a group of people I had recently met. One night, we were looking up at the stars in silence. I felt God's presence very clearly as we contemplated the vastness of the universe. I thought to myself, these moments are what life is about – vulnerability, wonder, awe, good company. These strangers I met in California came into my life and wrecked my heart in such a beautiful way. They got down into my grief with me in ways that people I'd known for years didn't. And they had never even met Courteney. One person in particular, named Henry, helped me learn to appreciate my strengths. He highlighted the gifts God gave me to share, pushing me to shine and radiate these truths. Being reminded by complete strangers that there is something that sets me apart helped me to fully own my gifts.

> *"I feel myself coming back-*
> *my free spirit self.*
> *I drew the house next to me,*
> *the way the sun reflects off the windows*
> *for 2 and a half hours in a sundress.*
> *I lost myself in the depth of the architecture.*
> *It felt like only 10 minutes had passed.*
> *I really don't need other people to complete me*
> *and that's a kick-ass feeling.*
> *Music started playing from the boathouse*
> *as the sky was painted orange.*
> *I was so present in the moment,*
> *I felt my heart open,*
> *my soul shivered.*
> *I'm so thankful for this opportunity to heal and disconnect.*
> *I feel at peace.*
> *I haven't had a moment*
> *where I've fallen in love with myself for a long time,*
> *but this is one.*
> *God is so good.*
> *I could see Him looking down*
> *smiling at His daughter*
> *as her eyes got wide*
> *and her heart danced*
> *with joy and gratitude.*

KATHERINE FLYNN PLUCINSKY

You know those moments
when halfway through laughing with someone,
you realize how much you appreciate their existence?
I had that with God.
And I had that with myself.
The world tries to complicate what we need to be happy,
but it's really quite simple.
Through God's pursuit of me,
I'm falling in love with myself again."
- journal entry

If you ever get the chance to disconnect with the world in order to reconnect with yourself, I urge you to take it. You deserve all the healing and peace in the world. You deserve joy dancing in your eyes and stomach ache laughter, and the right to let those tears fall and water the flowers beneath you. You deserve days of bliss and quiet too. You deserve to live life being free + open + healed. You deserve it all.

OPEN YOUR STILL-BLEEDING HANDS

(3 years)

A month before Courteney passed away, she told me that she got a calling for me to be a Catholic missionary on a college campus with an organization called FOCUS. I brushed it off at the time saying no thanks, but later I took her words to heart. So a year and a half after Courteney's accident - in her legacy - I did that for two years, walking with college students in their faith. It honestly makes me laugh that I thought I was going to be the one serving, making a change in the world. Yet, I'm the one who sits here - *changed*. God obviously had a lot of humility in store for me.

My heart was so hardened, I felt like I didn't have much to give. I wasn't sure about the idea of letting people close to me. Not after experiencing grief on such a raw level. Not after knowing what it felt like to love so deeply, and then to lose even more deeply.

My heart was in a slow and quiet process of unfolding ever since I said yes to God's call. Originally I thought God (and Courteney) made a mistake asking *me* to be a missionary, especially in Boise, Idaho. But apparently He knew the whole time. Because I'm sitting here, three years later, writing this as the sun is setting over a pond in Boise I had once hoped would be an ocean in California. I feel a deep gratitude overwhelming my being, because I have been t r a n s f o r m e d.

Nothing quite floods my heart like bringing people closer to God. Nothing. But I have learned more than I have taught. I have received more than I have given. I actually believe that God heals, and people heal. I don't know if I could've said that before, after experiencing the suffering and grief that this world holds. I was cynical of people, and I hate to admit it, but I was cynical of God.

But I know now. That forgiveness is possible. Healing is possible. Remaining soft after pain, although the more terrifying option, is possible. And not only possible, but it is immensely worth it. The pain of loving someone and then losing them, is worth it. And even after - to remain open, to remain vulnerable - is worth it. To live broken-open is so incredibly rewarding.

Despite the hurt, to open your still-bleeding hands to reach out to other people, but in return - to find them healing you.

You don't have to wait to be completely healed and no longer broken, to do that thing that you want to do because you may never arrive to that place, or at least in the way you expect. It turns out that the very thing that God is asking of us - the thing we feel inadequate for - will be what heals us. If I had remained closed, if I refused to believe that God could use my brokenness, if I refused to get out of myself and do something for someone else, if I refused to stop being a victim and being angry at the world for my pain, I would be in that same resentful, sad spot. I wouldn't have allowed God to get close enough to my broken heart to tenderly care for my wounds.

I learned that it's a journey, and you can find joy even before everything is resolved and known. The true joy is found in the process, rather than the destination.

I learned that success is measured not by productivity of the day, but by the degree to which we are present with what we're doing and who is in front of us. I learned that freedom is found in the loss of control, and although we crave control, it's a gift we don't have that kind of responsibility. God allows us to relish in simply being the creatures instead of the Creator. I learned that having a trusting + thankful heart actually gives us more peace than any control we could have. In the acceptance of having no idea what I'm doing, of not having the solution to every problem, and not having to pretend like I do, there is a release from the weight I carry daily. My poverty is freeing because the child-like dependency on God is stronger than my own strength will ever be.

God is God, and I am not
(and thank God I am not.)

I learned that honesty breeds honesty. Vulnerability breeds vulnerability. Life is too short to waste energy pretending to be something, if you don't feel it. It's better to invite people into the reality of where you are, and let them surprise you by loving you right there.

Life is too short to not have deep, meaningful conversations every single day. Life is too short to not talk about what's important, and what's hard. To bring the lies we believe about ourselves into the light, to invite other people into the parts of ourselves that feel most vulnerable, and to let ourselves be loved there and to love in return.

I learned that life is messy and although people may at times hurt you, *people will also be the very thing that will heal you.* I've experienced love from people in my life now in such a specific way that has healed wounds caused by people many years ago.

I came to know God so much more intimately simply because I grew weary of pushing Him away. I grew tired of pointing at Him, yelling at Him, blaming Him for my pain. Out of my own exhaustion and surrender, I stopped pushing. I stopped blaming, just long enough for Him to come close so that I could actually see the truth. He is not the reason for my pain, but rather the Physician for it.

I learned that God defends the heck out of my heart. He fights all of my battles - even the ones that I can't see. I must only remain still. He is not only with me, He is for me, on my behalf. And that is the same God that is for *you*. That fights for you. That calls you by name. That protects and heals your heart. As long as you remain open and let Him in long enough to do so. We need not be self-reliant. We can put down our swords, our defense mechanisms, the masks of being tough or "not caring," and we can just let Him defend our hearts for us, shamelessly.

I didn't know that when I said yes to being a missionary, I was actually saying yes to opening my heart again to people, to God, and to the world. If I knew that, I might have said no because that sounds unnerving. But in my yes, in getting outside of myself in love for the other, I found a path to abundant life.

A life of freedom + peace
inspiration + surrender
purpose + community
revival + passion
healing + restoration.

I'm grateful to the people who supported me financially and spiritually. A lot of the fruit we may never see until Heaven, but I can't wait to see it with you together in the Kingdom.

To Courteney's parents, I wouldn't have been able to fundraise without your help.

To Ralph, who bought me a car after Courteney's accident, thank you for leading me to a road of independence.

To the students I walked with, thank you. It was the joy of my life to run with you.

To my team, thank you. Specifically to my teammate Riley - for healing me with your love and friendship, for always speaking truth into my life, and for the ways you radiate Jesus just by who you are.

To my family, thank you for raising me with the values and beliefs I hold close today, for teaching me about God growing up, and for pouring yourself into my formation and making me into who I am.

And to God, thank you. You knew what You were doing all along. Please help me to trust you in this next chapter of my life. Even amidst all the uncertainties, I know You'll provide.

Teach me, God, to always remember that radiating Your light is a lifelong mission. For where You go, I will follow. I see now that wherever You call me is better than anything I can imagine for myself.

    Teach me to live with a heart
    b r o k e n - o p e n,
    for You.

    Teach me
    after being broken-open
    to never go back to living inside my safe, comfortable ways again.
    To never live the same way again,
    for my eyes are opened to a new depth of life.

FINGERPRINTS

 there's something about the things
that remain exactly as you left them.

your messy room,
the dirty laundry in your hamper
with your scent.
quickly-changed clothes on the floor,
your half-drank water bottle.
your planner - your handwritten schedule to a tee
weeks and even months
after your departure.
your half-conquered and partially crossed-off to-do list that stressed you out
filled with now-irrelevant tasks
of paying rent, returning shoes, and studying for tests.
your make-up bag with
on-sale tubes of concealer
and winter-colored palettes,
even though summer fills the air now.
your wallet - receipts and displaced dollar bills,
your fake ID that we ordered together
and you somehow managed not to get taken,
while i did not get so lucky.

these things are
  e x a c t l y
as you left them.

and to grasp that these things are still here,
but **you are not**.

the current feeling of them being
the "last-used"
of your daily necessities
makes me feel closer to you.
perhaps because, since these are the last things you used
and held,
and touched,
it feels that somehow
i
am also the last thing you touched now, too.

your fingerprints remain here
and the solace i find in the things that you left
-i n c o m p l e t e -
convinces me for a moment
that you'll be back
to finish them.
you'll be back
(i tell myself)
to do your laundry,
to pick up the clothes on your floor,
to drink the rest of that water,
and cross off the rest of your accomplishments for the week.

3 hours,
5 boxes,
and 0 boundaries later,
i find myself pretending these things
will bring you back
even just for a moment.

and then i remember your spirit
(your bright soul)
is more than your $25 matte lipstick
and your white patagonia sweatshirt,
the one i'm clinging to,
the last object that still holds your scent.

you are more
than your fingerprints.

UNCONVENTIONAL GRIEF

maybe you are
grieving,
without
shaking hands
with
death.

the loss of someone
or something.
a dream,
a relationship,
an idea,
the loss of normalcy
of what once was.

to grieve
what is alive,
beating,
+ breathing

to watch the slow deterioration,
the changing.
a slipping grasp
of what you once knew
and loved

this grief
is a certain kind
of stinging.

where
h o p e
lingers
with no intention
to deliver.

staying
far past
its welcome,
keeping you stuck,
holding on
to a reality
that no longer exists.

KATHERINE FLYNN PLUCINSKY

so although
you have not attended
a funeral,
be gentle
& soft
with yourself.
you are still
grieving.

you have still
had to say goodbye.
you have still
had to mourn.

you don't need
a death certificate
for validity
in your grief.

PART III:
IMPACT ZONE

"I was going backward, headfirst, upside down on my board, and in the lip of a 10-foot wave. It was absolute mayhem and violence. I was tumbling every which way like a piece of lint in a washing machine. It was pitch dark and I didn't know which way was up. The force and and power of the turbulence was like nothing else I have felt but that wasn't the worst part. The worst part was the complete powerlessness I felt as I was flailing, my arms trying to somehow swim out of this nightmare. The panic was starting to set in. How long is this going to last. I can't hold my breath much longer."

– Simon Short

THE IN-BETWEEN

it is dark
and lonely here.
you can't see much.
you have been emptied
of the old.
but not yet filled
with the new.
you have outgrown your old garden,
but you're not among the new bloom yet.

both directions
are fighting for your attention.
they sense the void
and want to fill it.

do you run back
to the comfort
of where you were,
because where you are going
seems uncertain still?

or do you remain
where you are?
do you wait it out,
breathing through,
holding onto patience
and trusting in blind-faith
that you will arrive
where you need to be
soon?

you have already done
the hardest part.
which is
d e c i d i ng
to replace where you were
for where you are going.

your destination
holds much more for you
than your starting point.

it has called you by name
with whispers of potential
and inflections of hope,
and you have already said
yes.

let that be your strength
as you move through the middle.
because this part
may be
the most important,
the most transformational.

it may be
your favorite part
of the journey,
if you let it.

roots grow underground,
babies form in the womb.
just because growth is not seen
does not mean it is not taking place.

hold on,
your
in-between
will soon be
your revival,
your new
b e g i n n i n g.

UNDERTOW

for so long
chaos has been
comfort.

chaos is
an old friend i've outgrown
but still pick up the calls
for being there for me so long.
although i am growing taller than chaos,
i attempt to shrink
to still fit in,
holding on
as though i owe something to it.

i'm finally learning that
to end chaos
is not to fight it.
because fire fights fire
and the flame is only fueled.

so get off the rollercoaster
and watch as it continues without you
buckled in.
it doesn't need your participation
in order to keep running.
if you're in it,
a part of it,
engulfed in the ride,
you've lost yourself.
you've become the ride.
you've become the chaos.

you can't fight it
while maintaining yourself.
you can't keep your
composure and character intact.
you are not above it,
and you will be lifted into the turbulence
like a bystander clinging

for your life
from a tornado.
so disengage,
do not respond,
do not meet chaos
where it is any longer.
you don't need to make excuses
for it to exist.

you don't owe an apology for disengaging.
you don't owe an explanation to anyone
who continues to get on the ride
of why you stopped paying.
of course they want you there,
it's scary to be on the ride alone.
but that is their choice
and you have yours.

and when your old friend
comes knocking on your door,
peek outside before you answer
and then close the curtains,
make some tea,
open a good book,
and sit in your peace.

you'll find new friends
to keep you company
when chaos isn't there to entertain
like it used to.
when it stops coming to the door
after enough times of not answering,
you will find better things to pour yourself into
like creativity
and spirituality.

in creativity,
you will find the excitement
without the fear.
inspiration will lift you up
and art will call you higher.

in spirituality,
you will find
the consistency
without the craziness.

you will discover
there is so much more
than yourself.
so much more
than the chaos.

GOOD FATHER

i'm 13.
in a moment of helplessness and desperation,
i cry out:
"God, i need you."

to this day – i still cannot accurately describe what happened in the moments to come
after I uttered this prayer in my heart.

God's arms
wrapped
around my entire being
and a divine force shield
suddenly surrounded me
in an embrace.
nothing on this Earth
could touch me.
and the deepest peace i've ever known
enveloped me
so fully
that it overtook
any ounce of fear and danger.
my soul seemed to elevate.
it was the safest i've ever felt.
this was my first personal experience with God,
my first glimpse into Heaven.

and from that moment,
i knew i had tasted Truth,
i knew it was real,
and i knew i wanted more.

my 13 year-old self
decided that night
that faith would be the most stable thing in my life.
it would carry me through things
i had no idea were coming.

some may call it foolish
that the thing that's been
the most constant + steady in my life
has been something
i've never been able to see or touch.
the thing that i center my life around
has been something
i have no hard proof or evidence of.

but that night,
i learned that i have a good, heavenly father.
i was aching for protection and stability,
and that night,
i found my *refuge*.

do we truly believe God to be good?

it is never His intelligence or capability we question,
rather the goodness of His heart and His concern for us.
it is not His power,
but His love.
His love, specifically for *us*.
that is where we doubt.

there is more emphasis placed on
the God of justice
than
the God of mercy.

we have to stop viewing God
as a strict slave master and rulemaker,
instead of the loving Father He is.
God is not a father of narcissism.
even if you didn't get to be a child growing up,
you get to rest in that now
and forever.

as long as you believe God doesn't care about your heart
and only wants to control your actions,
you are missing out on the reality of
a love that could change you forever.
you are missing out on **the** most
important relationship
you may ever have.

if we don't know God's individual love for us,
it is useless to "practice" religion.
if it is not deeply personal,
it is simply a ritual without any substance,
a title without any relationship,
and action without any purpose.

the heart of spirituality
is knowing and loving God
and God knowing and loving us.
& often we tend to distract ourselves with the rest.

a good father's only concern is for his children.
meanwhile a slavemaster's only concern is for himself and his power.
if we truly understood that God cares for us
way more than His own power,
we would come to trust in the goodness of His heart.
we would come to know His love for us in its fullness.
knowing that God is seeking our best interest, our dreams, and our peace
instead of living out of this fear of being controlled
or feeling like our "freedom" is being taken away.
that is why the prodigal son left home;
he wanted "freedom."
isn't that why we leave home, too?
we assume we know better than our Creator.

the prodigal son's homecoming
was the joyous celebration
of him realizing
all along
his freedom was back at home
with his father
who loved him unconditionally.

we are the prodigal son.
in our lives,
we leave often
and have multiple homecomings:
that random urge to pray,
that desire to get closer to God,
going back to church after years of having no interest,
realizing we need to turn away from something that is hurting us,
being drawn to silence and beauty,
that deeper *t h i r s t*.

how many times in a day
do we run away from God
seeking a freedom
that is already ours?

and each time we come back unfulfilled,
each time we return,
a banquet is held
in our honor.
every single time
we are celebrated.

experiencing suffering can dim our view
on the reality
of God's generous heart for His people.
i believed the lie
that because God was allowing my suffering,
it is what He wanted for me.
my jaded perspective only saw blessings as
"preparations"
because something bad was bound to happen sooner or later,
and i only got the good
to prepare me for the bad.

"i believe you desire my suffering, God," i pray,
"i don't want to think that, but i do.
show me who you actually are."

and God quietly shows up,
saying "daughter, I long to fulfill your desires.
to heal you. to love you. to give you peace."

every celebration of the mass,
we make a
d e c l a r a t i o n
of our healing.
we profess the words,
"Lord, i am not worthy
that you should enter under my roof
but only say the words
and my soul shall be healed."

and He does.
He says the words
e v e r y t i m e.

the same words that are
spoken to the sick servant
are spoken to you:
*"go, let it be done for you
as you have believed."*
the boy was healed
at that very moment.

the words spoken to you
are the same words
Jesus declares to the girl who died
but got up and walked when she heard:
"talitha kum"
which means
little girl -
a r i s e.

the words spoken to the woman with
a hemorrhage for twelve years
when she touched Jesus' clothes
reign true for you:
"daughter,
your faith has made you well.
go in peace and be healed
of your affliction."
these are your words of healing, too.
hold them close.

God weeps to see His children hurt.
He kneels down to our level,
in the suffering itself,
and holds us without letting go.

do we truly believe God weeps with us;
that He enters into our hurting in a real way?
or do we think God is distant?
do we believe Jesus sees our pain
and it literally moves him to tears?
do we believe that God knows in *every* moment
what our hearts need;
whether that's to ease the storm and give us peace,
or to let the storm rage on and let us cry + sit with us in it all?
my pain,
your pain,
is not distant or irrelevant to God.
it's very personal.

the Father's approval is all i long for in this life.

with me + with you
child,
He is well pleased.
He is with you.
He is good.

PERSEVERING LOVE

"why," he asked?
"for love," i answered.

"not in a cliche way,
but people give up on each other so easily.
       i don't care what someone does,
no one
deserves
to be alone
in this life.

   no one.

and for that reason alone
i will continue
to show up
for anyone
who needs it."

HENRY BROWN

i didn't know
the boy with blue eyes
sitting by himself
listening to jack johnson.

i didn't know
his inner battles,
his gentle heart,
or how contagious his laughter was.

as i sat next to him,
he handed me one of his headphones.

i didn't know
the boy with blue eyes.
but what i did know
in that moment
was listening to music
with this stranger
would change me.

his coming
and his going.
all of it
would change me.

my grief feels incomplete still,
unsure of how to talk about it,
and with whom.
unable to explain
how we healed each other
in unforeseen ways.
how to conceptualize
grief:
the very thing that brought us together
was just as quickly
the very thing that separated us.

i didn't know
the boy with blue eyes
but the morning of his friend's passing,
i couldn't help but embrace him

because that's all i ever needed.

*just to be held
and
space for my grief to be held.*

every morning i sat by the ocean.
in silence, we watched the waves,
his voice whispering,
"i hope you know you're as beautiful
inside
as you are out."

we spoke often about courteney
and the pain that came with losing her,
never knowing
one day
i'd lose him too.

how do you justify addiction
when someone is so committed to sobriety.
i questioned God
and free will
and why another beautiful soul
had to go so young and unexpectedly.

new years was the last time
we talked on the phone,

and then he was gone.

just like that --

as death reigns so permanent.

where is the closure
where are the answers
when it comes to addiction
when it comes to death.

i can't grasp
that he lost in a battle
that was so unfairly given to him
like it easily could've been handed to
me, or to you.

how could
the one thing

someone hates more than anything
be the one thing
that takes them away?
how could a substance
conquer
the resiliency of
a human being?

he always encouraged me to write,
so henry brown,
i'm following through with this.
these words are for you
and the life that you sought through.
you sowed many seeds of love
i wish you could see blossoming now.

from time to time,
i'll sing bravely
like you asked.
i'll even root for the seahawks
but in return,
Heavenly friend,
you have to root for me, too.

**To my sweet friend, Henry: I love you. Thank you for always encouraging me to pursue writing. Although addiction became too overwhelming, your spirit lives on in a thousand ways. The love of God you had and the love you showed me during such a hard time in both of our lives will always be something I hold close to my heart. I miss you so much.

**If you're struggling with addiction, please reach out. One relapse could take your life. I have so much respect for you and the battle you fight daily. You are a warrior. Don't give up.

COPING

you are not stuck.

not now,
not ever.

run

    write

        pray

            make tea

                explore photography

                    go for a drive

                        vent

                            blast your
                            favorite album

                      cry

                  go for a walk

            watch a documentary

          take a bath

      be outside

   do yoga

read

...
thank chaos
for teaching you
what calms your heart
and stills your soul
during a storm.

for knowing
there is always an option
to care for yourself
when it rains.
    and with so many
    outlets
    to choose from,
    ...
    none
    need
    to be
    d e s t r u c t i v e.

LOOK DEEPER

there are so many misunderstood layers
beyond
the substance itself.
in fact,
addiction has almost nothing to do
with the substance.
but rather the v o i d
the substance is filling.
and don't we all fill our voids?

when did we begin
standing on pedestals
shouting at others
for doing what we do
but for doing it
in a different way?

isn't God the only one
who can do such a thing?
and isn't God the only one
who chooses not to?

writing someone off
is not how you help them.
look deeper.
don't see the substance.
see
the pain,
the hurt,
the isolation.
these are the things
s h o u t i n g,
a c h i n g,
to be heard.
to be held.

remember
the opposite of addiction
is not sobriety,

but
c o n n e c t i o n.

look deeper.
love deeper.

Al Anon is an incredible resource if you love an addict.

PART IV:
SWIM AGAINST THE CURRENT

"Every time you think you are broken, know this: You are never really breaking. No one can break an ocean, darling. All you are doing is breaking the glass that is holding you back, diving deeper into your own depths, discovering yourself in pockets of the most somber waves, rebuilding your heart with coral, with seaweed, with moon colored sand dust. So stop trying to hold yourself back inside that glass. It was never meant to hold you. Instead break it, shatter it into a thousand pieces… and become who you were always meant to be, an ocean, proud and whole."

– Nikhita Gill

TAKE BACK YOUR POWER

f r e e yourself.

do not let words that ring of other people's insecurities
weigh you down or rob you of your peace.
do not let empty threats and hurtful deceit
cloud your reality or
take away your power.
do not allow anger to jump from them to you
like a spreading wildfire.
isn't that what anger wants after all?
to be contagious
and steal the place
of peace + joy.

do not let those words
make you hard or
make you feel small
but let them lead you into deeper compassion + genuine kindness
i n w a r d.
do not let someone's deafening disapproval
dim the light in your eyes
or the fire in your soul.
do not let someone else's hatred
make you bitter or cynical or closed off.

and if you carry anything with you,
let it be this:
a person can only meet you
as deeply as they've met themselves.

their words have
n o t h i n g
to do with you.

do not let someone else's blame
take away the things you know to be
utterly **good** and **true** about yourself.
for love is found in *freedom*,
not in guilt or shame.

radiant soul -
avoid the tragedy of
letting another person's words and actions

keep you from all the beautiful things
you're going to do in this world.

root yourself in the Truth,
dig your heels deep into Scripture.
let the Father's words of your beauty and belovedness
echo within your heart
and let *that* be your confidence.
allow yourself to rest in being childlike, and simple, and pure
and remain still,
because God is defending the heck out of your heart
even when you cannot see or feel it.

surround yourself with the people that see your soul,
the people that know your depths,
beautiful + messy,
and love you for it all.
embrace the people that hold a mirror back to you
like a lighthouse when you're lost at sea
guiding you back to who you are
& what you deserve
when you lose sight of it all.

and most of all,
do not get frustrated at your heart
for its vastness,
for its sensitivity,
for its fragile proof of being human.
do not kill off
your single greatest quality.

and although it may make you more susceptible
to absorb the emotion and pain around you,
it also gives you access
to an incredible well of empathy that you can draw from.
a more profound capacity to
both give + receive love in ways
that you didn't even know were possible.

remember
hatred speaks in a language that lacks substance.
as heavy as the words may be-
they are not
s u b s t a n t i a l.
they are not
sound, or worthwhile, or well-built,
and thank God: they are not urgent or valuable.

you deserve to have thoughts that are heard,
feelings that are witnessed,
needs that are met.
you deserve no's that are accepted,
and values that are respected.
and it's your responsibility to leave any place
where this isn't the truth for you.

your ability to trust yourself
& your sense of worth
is growing more and more firm
each day.
you're finding your footing.
you're standing
on less shaky ground.

because other peoples' chaos
ends where you begin.
so release,
exhale,
and be set free.
there is no need to
live out of fear.

it does not have power over you
any longer,
dear friend.

BRAVERY

gentle warrior:

in case no one has told you lately,
or you don't feel it

you exude bravery.

for doing that thing that feels uncertain to you.
for choosing the harder solution.

for acting towards your values
even if it means criticism
and pushback.

you are brave
for breaking patterns
and ending generational cycles.

even if the people you love most
get angry at you
for it.

for doing something different
and creating new normals.

you are brave
for moving.
for making action
- any action -
towards the life you want,
instead of the life you feel stuck in.

you are brave
for listening to your heart
even when false guilt
screams loud for your attention.

you are brave

for crying
    for feeling
        for screaming
            for reaching out
when it would be easier
to distract + numb.

because the way you handle this
cannot be judged
as right or wrong.
you're doing the best thing
in every moment.
and you are brave alone
for the mere fact
that you are experiencing
what you are.

you are courageous
for seeking therapy
and doing the work
that most avoid their whole lives.

for no longer letting
the avoidance of discomfort
or the fear of conflict
hold you in place.

you face fear
and exchange it for faith.
you confront shame
and return it for serenity.

you are brave
for staying
s o f t
& tender & gentle & loving
in a world that has tried
to make you hard.

your bravery comes
from simply
and continually
showing up.

each choice,
every decision,
towards bravery
is adding up.
so when you feel selfish
for taking care of your mental health,
remember
this isn't just for you.
people are counting on you.
your friends,
your family,
your future self,
your future partner,
your future children,
your future.

do it for you,
do it for them,
today.

(not all heroes wear capes,
but send me your address
because you sure as hell deserve one.)

TWENTY - THREE

i love twenty-three
because it's a year of red wine
and morning coffee-making before work.
it's a year of independence and heels.

but it's also a year of knowing my worth,
of finally deleting that text instead of responding
because twenty-three is the year i realized
that your validation does not change my existence.
your attention doesn't make my being
any more
or
any less.

you don't get to ask me how i am
when you haven't asked me all year.
you don't get to know my late night thoughts,
my realizations,
my beautiful encounters,
the chaos,
my daily happenings
any more.

you don't get to know what i've been learning,
and how i've grown,
and the ways that God has changed my heart.
you lost that privilege a long time ago
when you lost me.

you don't get to reach out when it's convenient for you.
you do not get to make me feel so insignificant
because i'm refusing to give you that power
any longer.

the truth is
moments with God will fill me
more than anything from you ever will.
moments in silence will make me feel more known
than an eternity of sweet talk you could utter.
when i experience beholding the King and Him beholding me,
it brings more peace
than your inconsistent arms ever could.

23 is the year of releasing,
turning the page,
and letting go.
it's the year of newness and excitement
for the joy and love ahead.
23 is the year i am free from you.
it is the year i am
my own.

CODEPENDENCY

you are not responsible
for making other people happy.
it is not your job
to rescue.
you can take off your badge
and your hat.
you are off duty
at least for a few moments
right now.

humility tells us
we don't have all the solutions.
humans are free
to have their own reactions,
and thoughts,
and feelings
     -    as am i -
and that is a birthright we were given
once we joined this life.
the beautiful thing is
what affects you so deeply,
that you take responsibility for,
actually has
n o t h i n g
to do with you.

we steal the independence of another
when we try to manage and change
what is happening
within them.
some things are necessary
to be felt
and it is not up to you,
and up to me,
to decide what should be felt
and what should be taken away
for another.
perhaps the anger
is just as important as the joy.
perhaps the sorrow needs to be felt
and mourned.
perhaps these very things

that we try to take away
are exactly what is needed
for a change to be made.

everyone always needs
something.
well i am here
to give you permission
because guilt is not allowing you.
i give you space away
from the fixing.
just a moment's rest
from the maintenance work
you busy yourself with
in other people's hearts.
i give you permission for silence
and a phone turned off,
to hear
what God is speaking to your soul,
and what you've been neglecting
within yourself.

i'm here to tell your guilt
to gently fuck off.

because your guilt isn't nearly as powerful
as you allow it to be.
and it doesn't have your best interests in mind.
it isn't willing your good,
dear friend.

when did you apply for this job,
when did you sign this contract,
that tied you down to a lifetime of
the humanly impossible task
of regulating
everybody else
internally and externally
to make sure that nobody
feels a damn thing,

except for you.
because you can feel it all,
you can handle it,
you'll be fine,
right?

but while you look out for everybody else,
who is looking out for you?
or was that part skipped over
in the agreement?
can you find it in the fine print?

hear me,
not just with your ears
but with your heart,
you are good.
repeat with me brother,
hear me sister.
you are good.
you are good.
as you are now.
as others are now.
as life is now.

enough cleaning up messes
you didn't make.
enough feeling bad
for taking care of yourself,
and then feeling bad
for yourself.
you're doing everything you have to
in order to survive.
you're doing the best you can,
and it's enough.

your needs are not
an ailment.
they are not scandalous,
or too much.
the people that love you
want to hold you after a long day.
they want to affirm you of the person you are,
but it is up to you
to recognize the need
and to vocalize it
in order to meet it.
there is no shame in needing other people,
in fact it is in our hardware.

if everyone else is allowed to need people,
allowed to need you -
shouldn't you be able to do the same?

I AM WATER

i am water.
you can stab me
over and over again
and i will still remain water.

you can take me from the sea
and gather me into a vase
but i will still remain ocean water.
nothing can take away my essence.

you can change my shape
but you can't change me.
i am fluid.
i am water.

flexibility,
adaptability,
& resiliency
have been gifts
as a result of
the always-shifting ground
beneath my feet.

the chaotic + the unknown
gave me character traits
that are serving.
i'm in gratitude
for learning elasticity
when life doesn't go my way
or things change.
i can adapt
as water does.

i am fire.
you can try to extinguish me
over and over again,
but you're going to be the one
that gets burned
while i remain passionate,
blazing,
unaffected.
i am fire.

i am wind.
you can strike me
over and over again,
but you'll go right through.
the wind does not become
more or less.
it may move directions
but it still occupies the same amount of space.
i am expansive.
i am wind.

i am earth.
you can break me in your hands
over and over again,
but i will remain whole.
i am grounded.
i am earth.

i am the elements
you are the elements
and we are a lot more resilient
than we even know ourselves to be.

each time
we are afflicted,
we come back even more enduring,
more unbreakable,
more whole
than before.

PART V:
LET GO

"The temptation is to panic, and fight, kick and scream, work your way out of its grip. But a seasoned surfer knows that at this moment when the wave is in control, the best thing for you to do is surrender. Let go. Go loose. Fighting only saps your energy and drains your most precious resource: oxygen."

– Liz Milani

ART OF SURRENDERING

I experienced a true detachment from my own will and plan, and the sense of freedom that came from the release has been incredible. Control is a false illusion. We don't have control over many of the things that consume our hearts and minds, but we worry anyways because it makes us feel slightly more in control and connected to the outcome. We create connections to these things because it feels safer to worry about them than to admit our powerlessness to them. Complaining about the cloudy weather won't actually stop the rain. We create an opinion about it because being connected to things greater than ourselves makes us feel less small and more in control.

Surrendering + trusting is truly an art. It takes constant awareness to truly master. It is not something you can just "feel" into existence, and it's difficult to practice because it's such an abstract concept. I've learned that trusting + surrendering is a **choice** we have to proactively decide *every day*. Especially the days when we feel like we don't trust God, we must choose to say it anyways.

God unclenched her little fists,
placed her hands in His.
declared she wasn't a rock, but a child.
my daughter, be free & be wild.

Physically opening my hands - while praying, in a hard conversation with someone, in the midst of anxiety, while I'm doing something I don't feel strong enough for - is a tangible reminder of the control in this life I beautifully don't have. God, take what you want and give what you want. I am open.

After years of practicing (and failing) at surrender, I'm finally at peace with my dependence on God. In our culture, being dependent on anyone is considered weak because we're taught that if we want our needs met, we need to do it ourselves. This has been projected onto my relationship with God. How can I trust that my needs will be met if I am dependent on someone other than myself?

My resistance to this childlike dependency has finally given way and I've felt a great release. The weight that I faithfully carried around has finally fallen from my shoulders. I don't want God's responsibility; no thank you. As scary as it is to know that much of life is beyond our control, it's also freeing.

You cannot surrender through doing. It comes through *being*.

"Rest" has become a bad word. If we're not doing, we are wasting time. We have learned to measure the success of our day by productivity, not by the degree of presence we have to ourselves and one another. In my pursuit of surrender, I have found it most in the place of rest. By rest, I don't mean sleeping or checking out by binging Netflix. I mean silence, solitude, and awareness of God's presence.

The closest I am to God is when I just am; when I'm not trying to plan or control or hold it all together, but when I'm simply being. When I let down my walls and allow my feelings to surface. My heart spills out and I sit there with it all. I look at my fears and desires, gather the mess of my mind and heart and say, "take this God, have it all; it's too much for me." All I need to do is be still and You will fight my battles for me. You are stronger than any fear, lie, or desire fighting for my attention.

God allows us to rest in our childlikeness and doesn't expect anything in return, especially on the days when we feel like we have to earn His love, the days when every ounce of our being is clinging, grasping, and white-knuckling to what we think will make us happy. God sees how weary we get from trying to play a role that we are not capable of playing and He wants to remove that responsibility. He says, "Let me take care of it for you. Give it all to me."

Being part-introvert, my soul craves this kind of rest. At the end of a beautifully exhausting day, I like to pour myself a glass of red wine or a cup of mint tea. I open the window and listen to the rain. In these moments, I close my eyes and sit in awareness of God's presence. I feel fully known. In a world that tells us the solution to everything is more self-love, I have come to realize that finding real love doesn't come from focusing on the self. That has led me to emptiness, instead of deep fulfillment.

It took me 25 years to realize that I feel most connected to myself when my gaze is taken *off* of myself.

The more I am connected to God, the more I am connected to myself. The more I fall in love with God, the more I fall in love with myself. The two are far more intertwined than I realized, because by knowing the Creator of my heart, I come to a deeper understanding of my own depth and I start to see myself through His eyes, which is my truest self. I've become more aware of the way He sees me. The way He sees my heart dancing with gratitude at a sunset or a stranger's smile because He created me as a lover of little things. When I spend time with God, I have a greater awareness for what really makes my heart sing.

The truth is, things never happen as we plan. We lose people we'd never expect to circumstances we could never anticipate. But we also experience the unexpected blessings that come to us on the paths we never imagined ourselves taking. The growth, the healing, the incredible people I've met along the way. It's clear that He knows us better than we know ourselves. He knows what will fulfill our hearts better than we do because He fashioned them Himself. Why would I even try to control my life's story when I know that God is writing it perfectly, as we speak?

Surrendering is a *process* and it never really leads to a final destination. As cliché as it sounds, I have begun to find so much beauty in the process itself. I have a tendency to constantly be looking ahead at what I need to fix and work on next, but over the years, I've learned to be patient with where I'm at, in this moment, and to stop and celebrate that as a small victory.

Today I feel like I can say I trust God. Tomorrow I could be surrounded by doubt all over again. But for this moment that I can surrender, I am thankful.

I will continue to release the things that no longer serve me until surrender becomes my natural state of being, and in this will be freedom. True surrender has a way of creating an inner readiness to turn the page, to embrace this season of newness in my life. And even as it steadies me on my journey into the future, it also allows me to feel closure and peace with the gut-wrenching sadness and anger that were a part of the past.

We owe it to ourselves to feel our emotions as long as necessary. But at this moment, it no longer feels necessary.

Surrender makes room for new adventures, new love, and new friendships. Through this dependence on God alone, I've been freed from the need of external validation because God fills my soul more than any amount of people ever could. This has allowed for a refreshing simplification of my life and a new wholeness in my being.

All thanks to the **art of surrendering**.

Father,
you are not a God of suffering.
you want goodness for me.
you want healing for me.
you want me to find peace and joy.
you weep with me when i am suffering.
you don't want me to experience these things.
i'm sorry for not trusting in your goodness for so long.

God, grant me the patience to accept where i'm at.
my instinct is to fix, but allow me to be okay as i am;
because that is where you want me.
let me be okay in the midst of my healing process -
with the messiness of not being fully healed.

let me accept that sometimes it feels too much to be there for others
because i barely have the energy to be there for myself -
to be okay with not having the answers or solutions
but being able to offer my presence alone to another.

KATHERINE FLYNN PLUCINSKY

defender of my heart,
lover of my soul,
allow me to embrace the process.
to rest where i am
without looking at what's next,
to see the lengths i've come,
to make this journey my own
without worrying about the way i'm told it should look.

i give myself permission to be here,
to be 25,
to be grieving,
to not have all the answers.
i give myself permission to mess up,
to fail with other people,
to fail with myself.
i'm not where i want to be yet,
and i'm okay with that.
i have the rest of my life to get there.
So Father, thank you for where i am today.
because for today - it is enough.

i hear you promising good things.
and even after all the blessings and goodness
you have already brought into my life,
i still fall into doubt.
oh me of little faith.
i'm sorry for doubting you,
for not believing that you are listening to and protecting me,
and working on my behalf at all times.
you have been the most constant thing in my life,
you've never failed me
+
you won't start now.

Amen.

EMPTY YOURSELF

lord, make me a <u>channel</u> of your peace.

to be a channel
you must have a clear opening,
a space in which
life is allowed to flow through you.

d e t a c h m e n t.
where freedom
is born.

Fire Within, by Thomas Dubay, has an entire chapter dedicated to the freedom of detachment.

because God has given us free will, He allows us to choose what we fill ourselves with.
if we are filled with things of this world, there is simply no room for God to abide.
God can only come to us to the extent that we are uncluttered.
God respects what we want,
so if we want the world,
then He allows us to fill ourselves with it.
He will not move into a space where He is not invited.

Dubay says, "it is the pure of heart that sees God,
the single minded person who seeks the things above, not those on earth.
this heart is sensitized to the Holy Spirit, His enlightenments, movements, and enkindlings."

so, on the other side of
b r e a k d o w n s
are
b r e a k t h r o u g h s.

we lose that job,
we get that diagnosis,
we wake up to hundreds of
missed calls about our best friend's death.

in these life-shattering moments,
we realize that we can no longer place our identity
in our accomplishments,
our grades,
our relationships,
or the job we worked so hard to get.
we could even win the nobel peace prize,

and it still wouldn't matter
when these moments happen,
we somehow know that there's more
to who we are.

we are swiftly made aware of what matters
and what doesn't.

when the things we cling to so tightly for our security
come crashing down,
life is handing us an opportunity.
an opportunity to reclaim our identity.
we have no choice but to take it.
it's the shattering of our
i-centered life,
the one we create for ourselves.

the undoing.
the falling apart.
the breakdown.
the stripping.
the purifying.
the emptying.
then the breakthrough.
God waits for us there.

we are given the gift to choose again,
a chance to put our identity in something infallible,
rather than placing it back into another worldly outlet
that will sooner or later come crashing down
again, and again, and again.

if we live completely self-willed,
eventually we crash + burn.
i know this from my many attempts and failures.

Dubay says, "when God finds us open and ready, He cannot *refrain* from filling us to the extent that we are emptied."

for years, i wondered why God chooses to enter some hearts
more deeply than others,
even when the desire is very much there.
for a long time, i felt like i had to water down my love for God.
i felt guilty that i had experienced God, while other people hadn't.
they would ask me why they hadn't felt God when they prayed,
but when i read Dubay's words in *Fire Within*, i got chills and put the book down.
 it made so much sense.

"God fills us to the extent that we are emptied."

if we are completely filled up,
then it's no wonder why God can't come to us in a fully expressed way.
there is simply no room.

if that's the case,
then
God, i pray -
empty me of everything so there is nothing but space for you to reside.
empty me of my fears and my uncertainty about the future.
empty me of my obsession for pleasure and fleeting success.
empty me of my craving to be being liked and approved.
empty me of the pain i can't let go of
because of fear of who i would be without it.
free me of everything
except You.
let it all come crashing down.
may i be wholly focused on Your presence + will.

emptying ourselves is not a once-and-for-all thing.
it's an everyday choice that we need to consciously make.
even if we chose to empty ourselves yesterday,
the ego, the self,
has already built an entirely new empire within
today.

every morning
we must let it fall
and collapse to ashes
so that we don't become attached.
that space is for God
and what He desires.

this is what happens
when i receive the Eucharist.
my heart becomes a house,
and i allow Him to move in.

and this is why i'm so drawn to
brokenness,
rawness,
and rock bottoms -
these are places where life forces our hand,
and we have nothing but empty space.

fragility and weakness become a gift
because in them
we have no option but dependence.

when this happens,
detachment follows.
after eating a steak,
a hot dog just doesn't cut it.
and once you get a taste of God's love,
the world itself releases its grip.
at that point you know something much greater,
something that is truly fulfilling -
overwhelmly so.

nothing on this earth can completely satisfy us,
and if you are even slightly aware of the human experience,
then you know exactly what i'm speaking of.
i remember first noticing this emptiness in high school,
and watching myself and others try to fill it.

many people spend their whole lives trying to fill that space.
ultimately, they remain stuck
in their own disappointment.

but have you ever considered that maybe
this emptiness
is meant to be just that:
empty?
perhaps we aren't supposed to fill it.

if you placed furniture in every inch of your home, you'd constantly be bumping into your own belongings.
it would feel claustrophobic.
if books had no margins and words completely filled the page, you'd get a headache from trying to follow along.
if your plate was always full, you'd quickly lose your appetite.
empty space is necessary,
so let it be without filling it up
(with people, or money, or validation.)

instead of trying to frantically fill,
remain open.
on some days this will require maintenance
and you'll need to go in with cleaning supplies
and scrub the dirt away.
you'll need to open a window

and let some fresh air in.
and on other days you might need to go in with a hammer
to break down and smash
everything that is unnecessary.

once that is done,
keep this space sacred and open.
lay down a beautiful rug
so you can sit,
and invite God to join you.
this time,
you'll have the room for Him.

lord, make me a <u>channel</u> of your peace.

CHILDLIKE

if God is like father,
then we are like child.

there's so much to learn
and even more to *unlearn*.

the loss of compassion,
the loss of simplicity.
when did we begin
to dim our excitement
and stifle our expression?

we must unlearn
what we know
in order to learn again
how to live in a state of curiosity
instead of a state of fear.
to be present,
instead of anxious.
to play outside
until it gets dark,
and to lose track of time.
how to say exactly what we think,
to cry when we're sad,
to dance when we're happy,
and to ask for help when we can't reach
the top shelf.

how to fall asleep
when your mom scratches your arms,
allowing yourself to drift into a dream state
while listening to words sung about some place
over the rainbow.

how to feel everything
from the grass beneath your bare feet
to the intense anger of someone stealing your belongings.
never concerned of what other people will think
about your full expression,
the silliness of your excitement.

proudly showing off your talents in public.
doing a cartwheel

whenever you feel like it,
just because.

there's no pride,
no ego.
space to be simple
and space to dream.

words from the mouth
of my
eight-year-old self:

"the moon & the sun love me so much,
they follow me wherever i go."

may she continue to teach me
the joys of being childlike.
may she look up into the sky
and remember that she is loved
and cared for,
by even the most powerful forces
circling our earth.

REST

"if i only have the energy to be there for one person today, it's going to be you."
-me, finally choosing myself

you don't need to earn rest,
darling.

you don't need to justify and validate
- even to yourself -
what is already
always yours.
you don't need to do something useful
to justify your existence.

rest is not a reward
that can only be accessed
once you reach a certain
threshold of work,
once you convince yourself
that you are deserving.

bubble baths
and chocolate cake
float on the surface
of the ocean that is
self-love.

dive deeper
and say no to that thing you don't want to do.
and when the guilt comes up,
find that consoling voice
you lend so quickly to everyone else
to make it okay.

set boundaries
and walk away from the things
that you would not want the precious child in you
to experience.

self-love doesn't always feel good,
especially
if you're doing it right.

because self-care is not just
indulgence,
it's the letting go of
the things that are imprisoning you.

love is to will the good of the other.
so self-love is willing good
for yourself.

it's knowing yourself
inside + out,
so you can choose
what is best for you
in every moment that unfolds.
to know what your soul is craving
and then to follow that,
despite the opinions of others.
to know your needs,
and then meet them.
and when you can't,
to ask for help
so others can.

it's to trust yourself
that your mind and body
know what you need
and are always working on your behalf
to heal you,
to keep you alive.

walking into a counselor's office
two weeks after my best friend died,
i followed the question: "why are you here?"
with "to make sure i grieve properly."

as if grieving is
similar to holding your knife a certain way
at a fancy restaurant.
god forbid,
i grieve outside of the lines.

little did i know,
that i was going to grieve in whatever way

i needed to in each moment.
and that there is no proper way,
no wrong manner,
no way that i could've messed up.

i didn't know
before i met grief
how much my mind and body look out for me
in every situation.
i underestimated them greatly;
how much they know
what is best for me.
i've come to trust them
as a compass and map,
above any expert.

energy feels scarce
while your mind and body are grieving
and that's okay.
because love is both
mary and martha.
it's preparing a meal for your Beloved,
and it is also sitting at their feet.
love is being
as much as it is doing.
and if you don't have the energy to do
then love through being.
love through presence.
being present is all that love
asks of us
anyway.

choosing your own good
is to know
if saying no for a night of solitude and silence
is what you're needing,
or if it's actually better for you
to push yourself to do something
out of your comfort zone,
even if you aren't in the mood.

knowing if it's better
to drink that extra coffee
to complete the tasks of the day,
or if you need gentleness with your exhaustion
and to simply try again tomorrow.

this is something grief taught me.
to trust what i need in each moment
and to accept that.
to listen to myself
instead of the recommendations of others.

to know when to push myself,
and when to let myself rest.
to be okay with the days i might not get done what i need to
because frustration
won't make us more productive.

although you see weakness
and shame,
for drinking too much
and sleeping too long –
God sees a heart that's tired,
a heart that's still trying,
a heart that's showing up
right now.
a heart craving rest.

LET PEOPLE BE THERE FOR YOU

you don't have to do it on your own.
this life is not meant to be conquered
alone.

proving your independence
will not make you any happier.
you have already established
that you're strong enough
time and time again.
it's time to humble yourself
to r e c e i v e
and admit the very necessity
of needing people.

you have people in your life
that *want* to be there for you.
they want you to call them
when you're upset,
they want to know
what's going on,
they want to listen.
they want to love.

although there were people who weren't there for me through grief -
the people that *were* there for me and i couldn't see,
to them, i'm sorry.
to them, i love you.
to them, thank you.

i forgot to recognize
the ones who were there for me
because i was too angry
at the ones who weren't.

i became caught up
in my own dramatic narrative,
i wasn't aware
of all you did
behind the scenes

just for me
to get out of bed.

so the ones who have been there all along:
know this:
even when i felt cynical of people as a whole
and perhaps took it out on you,
i wouldn't have made it
without your loyalty
and persistence and love.
the way you didn't give up on me
no matter how many times i isolated,
losing sight of the very gift you are to me.
thank you for all you did
even when it felt thankless.

and thank you for showing me
during the hardest time in my life,
that people will be there.
that it's okay to need others.
that it was okay to need you.

and in the future
it's okay
if you end up needing me, too.

REMAIN GROUNDED

move the body
to still the mind.

walk.
notice.
be.

the way your feet feel hitting the earth
carrying the weight of your body.
vines coming out of the ground,
and gently forming around your feet
growing flowers around them.

being grounded
while *b l o o m i n g*.

watch as breath
slows time.

your jaw unclenches,
your shoulders drop.
you release into a spiritual space.
God is here.
God is always here
but now you're
a w a r e
that God is here.

notice what you see,
what your eyes seem to focus on,
what you feel drawn to.

what usually bothers you
d i s s i p a t e s
as you experience the moment before you.

God's face is in each person that passes.
you can't help but smile
as you are filled with adoration for each human that drifts by.
we are all connected.
the couple holding hands,
the man walking his dog,
the family laughing as they pass.

there is so much beauty and goodness
in humanity
because each of us has a light burning within;
God dwelling among us.

the woman rollerblading
pushing her husband's wheelchair
so his waist-down paralysis
does not inhibit
feeling wind rush against his face.

notice thoughts
then let each one pass
with no more or less
weight
than the one before it.
no judgment around
"good" or "bad."

listen to your thoughts
to discover that they are just that:
t h o u g h t s.
              then you can listen more closely
                      to God.

you will notice
the different tones.

rooted in love,
not judgment.
rooted in peace,
not insecurity.
simple truths.
encouraging.
grounding.

HOLY HOUR

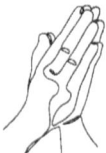

what's one habit that has been
monumental
in changing your life?

working out?
reading?
waking up early?

everything changed when i began
praying in silence for one hour everyday.

i had no idea how many things God desired to share with me
& all of the things He wanted to do in my heart,
but i was never giving Him the space or time to do it.
it was like asking a question
and walking away before hearing the response.

it's easy to develop a belief that God only loves us for what we do for Him -
but He actually just wants **us**.
He wants our hearts.
He wants me,
and He wants you.
(yes, even all of those messy parts... actually, especially those parts.)

at first, an hour of prayer felt like an *eternity*
but it has come to be the thing that fully roots + grounds me.
if i don't prioritize that in my day,
everything feels off.

if i check my phone
before talking to God,
i will lose myself
before i even get out of bed.
i'm less present to everyone and everything around me
and i become unaware of God's continual presence throughout the day.

prayer is where i find my deepest identity + security.
this beautiful dependency on God has become my joy

because if we have a God who is beside us in every moment -
what do we have to fear?

i think a lot of times, we get caught up in the how-to,
the rights + wrongs
but there is no right or wrong way to pray.
prayer is simply
y o u r
own relationship with God.
it's not about doing anything specific
or the structure of words,
but rather the openness of your heart.
don't listen to those who tell you
that you're doing it wrong,
because you simply can't.
it's a matter of being
rather than doing,
so how can you *be*
in a way that is wrong?

i love learning how different people
experience and connect with God
because it leads to a more expansive perspective of who God truly is.
i only have my own personal experience of God,
so in listening to others
i get a glimpse into His grandiosity.
our human minds can only conceptualize so much
because God is immensely more than we can even know or imagine.

and what a beautiful adventure this life is,
what a gift to continue unveiling the great mystery.

hearing the ways God speaks to you
specifically,
uniquely,
personally.
and the beauty of it being completely different
from how He speaks to me.

journaling is my favorite way to pray
because God created a deep love for writing in me;
how unique to my own heart.

He speaks loudly (or quietly),
through nature (or music),
through peace (or joy),
to each person based on who they are and how He created them.

& it is the most beautiful thing in the world to me
that no two people have the same relationship with God
because no two people have the same exact heart.

and
spoiler alert:
prayer may not always look "*holy.*"
as much as i want my relationship with God to be
the pinterest-perfect-pretty-highlighted-bible-God-is-good-all-the-time
kind of relationship,
it's not always like that

and that's okay.
because prayer isn't a feeling.
prayer is a relationship with God,
and relationships are messy.

if prayer is condensed to a feeling,
then the discipline to show up every day
+ persevere
is going to fade quickly,
as soon as the feeling fades.
just because you don't feel anything
doesn't mean God is not there.
the feelings you have about God
are not God.
the thoughts you have about God
are not God.
God is God.

consolation + peace + good feelings
are the grace that God gives
from time to time,
but they are not a measurement of
His presence.
because God is ever-present
even when the feelings are not.

what are we truly putting our faith in?
our feelings or God?

faith is more than our senses.
His presence exists
with, or without,
our approval and awareness.

prayer can be intimidating.
it's hard to feel like you aren't being heard
or there's no one there.
i've been praying for the same thing for a decade now
and still haven't seen the results i desire.
it's hard to feel like God is absent
in the presence of a battle.
but the purpose of a relationship with God
is not to get what we want.
we have a relationship with God
because of who He is,
and as humans we were created for
this relationship.
God is at the root of our every desire -
to be accepted,
known,
seen,
loved.
i'm completely and utterly restless
until i rest in Him.

sometimes prayer for me is silent + dry.
sometimes my mind is scattered and gets pulled in by all the things i have to accomplish.
sometimes it's me ugly-crying in the chapel trying to make sense of this life.
or sometimes it's me cussing God out, mad at the suffering the people i love have to go through.

and then after periods of anger and doubt and wrestling,
i come to a place of feeling like i have nothing left,
and there's no choice but to surrender.
to sit there empty-handed and choose to trust,
despite my lack of understanding
and the lack of validation that i crave.
my soul turns to the Father in all its need and says,
"you take care of it,"
then closes its eyes and rests.

& sometimes these are the most intimate, and raw, and spiritual things.
sometimes what we think is the least "holy" is actually
closest to the very heart of God.

showing up every day:
that's what it's about
just like developing any good habit.
no matter what i'm feeling or what my mood is,

no matter what the circumstances of the day have entailed,
i have to show up.
like any relationship, it takes work
and some days you don't feel like it.
but i know for me,
those are the days i need prayer the most.
those are the times my soul is yearning to fall on its knees.
to come as i am, feeling incomplete and to rest and be filled by the only thing that will truly satisfy my heart.
and to be received and loved for all of the messiness of my wonderful and imperfect human condition.

God has shown me time and time again
that when i trust Him and what He is asking of me,
i will never be let down or unfulfilled.
and not only will i not be let down,
but it is actually better than anything i could ever imagine for myself.

so my challenge to you, friend,
is to place yourself before God
and just be.
you don't have to do anything.
you don't have to be anyone.
you are enough as you are
right now.

on the other side
of this deeply personal relationship
with a God who loves us,
we find abundant life.

what are you waiting for?

for ten minutes,
close this book,
open your hands.
and get ready to receive.

let God surprise you.

SOFT DAYS & EASY BREATHS

inhale.

fear does not need
to determine our schedules.
we can live our days with ease,
instead of resistance.

how easy it is
to justify our suffering
saying, the Lord wants me here.
but does He?
there may be a level of
suffering + loneliness
that happens beyond our control,
even daily,
and it's beautiful to offer that up.
but if we have the choice
to be in a place of anxiety, fear, and suffering
rather than a place of peace and joy -
do we really think God wants us to choose
that anxious place?
our God is loving -
speaking truth that sounds like
"*be not afraid,*"
and "*my peace is with you.*"

we can grow
as much in the calm
as we can in the struggle.
we don't need
to always weather
the harder option,
the more tumultuous path.

our best lessons
don't only come
through tears,
but perhaps in our quiet mornings,
the light pouring in through the windowsill,
our sleepy sundays.

it's okay to choose
the release of an exhale
and road trips filled with laughter and friends,

instead of tight shoulders
and the rigid trek uphill, alone.

hold.

is life heavier
because i offer
to carry
more than i can?
because i heroize
the fight, the struggle?

do i add weight
because i focus on
the hard
and the heavy?

we waste our lives
chasing storms
and then
agonizing over the rain.
when instead
we could be
devoting our days
to soaking in the sun
and swimming in the sea.

maybe life
is not meant
to be taken so seriously.
maybe we are not
that
big of a deal.

it's okay to choose soft days
and easy breaths.

exhale.

PART VI:
STAND UP & RIDE

"Where but the moment before was only the wide desolation and invincible roar, is now a man, erect, full-statured, not struggling frantically in that wild movement, not buried and crushed and buffeted by those mighty monsters, but standing above them all, calm and superb, poised on the giddy summit, his feet buried in the churning foam, the salt smoke rising to his knees, and all the rest of him in the free air and flashing sunlight, and he is flying through the air, flying forward, flying fast as the surge on which he stands. He is a Mercury — a brown Mercury. His heels are winged, and in them is the swiftness of the sea."

– Jack London

21 YEARS YOUNG

dear younger self (21),

it's been a while since i've talked to you -
really since i started grieving.
i pushed you away
with my anger, envy, and resentment
for the way that you can live so naive and so freely.

what i want to tell you
all these years later is
i'm sorry.

it's not your fault that you didn't know what was coming
and the way it was going to change your life, and who you are.
it shatters my heart
for all that was taken from you
at just 21 years old.
not only was your best friend stolen from you,
but so was the innocence of your life perspective.
i couldn't look at you
without an overwhelming weight
of life's unfairness.
i could weep a thousand years
for all that was taken from you.
it made me too angry to feel -
so instead i stopped looking at you.

the way you see people beautifully,
each person in front of you as a gift to explore and to learn from
instead of as a weapon that could hurt you.
the way you trust,
even when it isn't the safest choice.
the way you don't even know yet
that pain + suffering + loss
e x i s t
at such a level and intensity.
the world you live in seems
vastly different from the one i live in
so i need you to remind me of a few things.

like how to dance around the living room again
and laugh for no reason at all.

how to let myself feel joy
without feeling guilty for it.

teach me again
(younger self)
to not worry about the person who didn't answer my call
knowing nothing bad happened to them,
they're just out running errands.

without the doubt that promises won't be kept,
without wondering who is going to leave or die next,
without having to be on guard
all of the time.
without being consumed with the fear of abandonment
or if people around me
can handle the weight of what i'm dealing with.

teach me again
to wake up inspired and passionate
about the adventure the day ahead holds.
the excitement about how God will use you,
about who you will meet,
and what good things will happen to you,
and how you can find ways
to make the world around you better.

and dearest friend, please teach me again
of what it looks like to not be tired,
to not feel defeated,
and to believe in the goodness of it all.
to be free to live in a way
where you don't expect anything to be taken from you,
where you don't have to live clinging so tightly
and locking your heart in a box
being mad at its vast ability to love
out of fear of losing
what is most important to you,
once again.

teach me more
than simply surviving.
to stop using all the energy i have on deciding
who and what to let in
and who and what to shield myself from.

HIGH TIDES & OPEN HANDS

teach me of what it means again
to not know panic attacks + anxiety + depression.
to have the seemingly endless flow of energy you have naturally
and to not only help people
but to do so with complete joy and zero resentment
for them taking what feels so scarce
that i barely have enough for myself.
teach me again to live in abundance and generosity.

teach me to drive up to the mountains blasting happy music with the windows down,
to let joy come in and stay for a while.
to forgive without retaliation.
to stay, and not to run
from the good things meant for me.

– and then sweet girl, let me teach you a thing or two –
like how to pray for an hour in silence everyday,
to let go of friends that you've outgrown,
and boys that have nothing to offer you.
to have better boundaries for yourself,
and to not let other people's opinions determine what you do
and the path you pursue.

i'm really proud of you,
and i hope you're proud of me too.

i love you endlessly,
 (25)

KATHERINE FLYNN PLUCINSKY

FALL IN LOVE WITH BEING ALIVE

"Promise me you will not spend so much time treading water
and trying to keep your head above the waves
that you forget, truly forget, how much you have always loved to swim."

- Tyler Knott Gregson

i've always been a
l o v e r
of the little things.

i fall in love
every day.
with strangers,
the way they become consumed with what they're working on,
and what they're reading.
how we happen to be in the same place
at the same time
to escape from our different lives.

the cozy feeling
of streets around christmas time
with lights draped around trees
and snow sparkling with every step.

the way the creamer
dances in my black coffee
like an afternoon storm
rolling through the sky.

i have moments when
i fall in love with myself, too.

running into the ocean,
my wet hair naturally curls
and the salt washes the make-up from my eyes.
my skin is warm and covered with sand,
and i'm overwhelmed with gratitude
that i am
who i am.
i love my thoughts,
and the way i love.

i fall in love with being alive.
i fall in love with it all.

the *process* of the first cup of coffee in the morning,
the sound, the smell,
the wait, the silence of the morning.

the pour of red wine
and dancing with friends.

watching the sunrise
from a rooftop.

white covers,
him asleep next to me,
sunlight dancing through the curtains
on a sunday morning.

i romanticize brunch,
and dressing up.

snorkeling under clear water,
with only the sound of my breath.
beams of sun striking through the water,
and fish of every color underneath me.

a coping skill
maybe,
a survival technique
perhaps.
to be enamored with the little things
and to let myself fall in love daily.
beauty capturing my attention.
recognizing truth + goodness
to slip away from the heaviness of life.
God sprinkles Himself
throughout the day.

when a sunset takes my breath away,
i sit in that moment for as long as possible.
when i race to my camera
so i can capture the sky in a given moment
because it evokes a feeling within me
that i hope to not forget.

even now,
as i'm sitting here in this cute little shop
in the heart of denver,
surrounded by strangers

and art
and a lavender latte,
listening to a piano track by sufjan stevens -
i've fallen in love
with this *moment*.

as my fingers swiftly type on my keyboard
in the same way
sufjan's fingers swiftly move across his.
using his hands
to create,
as i am doing here now.

different platforms,
same tempo.
and how i'm in love with this musician
i've never even heard before.
his ability for creation,
his state of flow,
that elevates me
to enter mine.

life is art.
we are art.
the way you dress, the way you create,
the way you can't help but close your eyes
and scrunch your nose
when you're laughing
is art.
the way you bite your lip
and your chin quivers
when you're about to cry
is art.
the way your heart aches
when you see someone experiencing homelessness
or when someone disrespects someone you love.
that is art.
what moves you
is poetry.
the learning about yourself,
about other people,
about places,
about this world,
it never ends.

you are the creation,
and when you create,
you become like the C r e a t o r.

the joy
the Creator experiences
when you sing with the voice
He fine-tuned you to have,
or your hand holds a brush
the same way as when He paints the sky
for your very eyes,
alone.

when you mimic God by taking clay
and molding your favorite vase,
the same way He took clay
and molded you,
with your ears that you worry are too big
and your patience that you worry is too small.

but when i see you sitting across from me
at a restaurant,
or driving in your car,
or at the airport,
i do not notice your ears for their size.
i notice the beauty of your eye color
and the way you seem to radiate with joy.
i don't even know you
- but i don't need to know you -
to recognize the beautiful creation,
the heavenly captivation,
that you are.

if we looked up,
we might be surprised at the art in every corner
of our lives
as if we're walking through a different museum
every day.

stop being afraid to call yourself
a musician,
a writer,
an artist,
or a cook
because you fear you do not qualify.

KATHERINE FLYNN PLUCINSKY

this life is art,
and you are both a creator
and the creation.

ACCEPTANCE

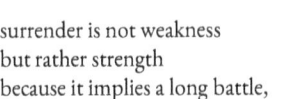

surrender is not weakness
but rather strength
because it implies a long battle,
a hard fight.

as i was leaving the cemetery on a random thursday afternoon,
i felt a deep sense of trust in God and His plan -
while s i m u l t a n e o u s l y
having the human experience
of a gut-wrenching emptiness in my chest,
a stinging blend of anxiety and depression
that has remained just as strong since day one.
tears of the deepest sorrow
and raging anger were falling from my eyes.

surrender does not equate to feeling good about everything.

although when i picture surrender,
it's running in a field of sunflowers
with arms wide open,
laughing, full of joy and freedom –
not 25-year-old katherine driving home from the cemetery
crying so hard she can't see the road
and full of angry thoughts.

yet, here we are.

surrender does not have to be coming to good terms with the unfair
and cruel traumatic events that have taken place in your life.
it doesn't need to erase all negative emotions.
you might still feel angry –
it doesn't mean you aren't trusting and surrendering.
you can still wish it didn't happen,
and you can still not understand.

but
amidst everything –
the anger,
the sadness,
the unfairness,
the questioning, doubting, and yelling –

to *still* trust and surrender.
to *still* choose to accept that God has a bigger plan than we can even fathom -
even if on a physical and emotional level, that feels false.
to *still* choose to believe that God's knowledge far surpasses our own -
even when we feel like things would be so much better if they had gone our way
and we were the one in charge.

the essence of s u r r e n d e r :
jesus's arms stretched wide on the cross
hands open,
giving up his self-will
for the Father's.

this is faith.
it is not the absence of human emotion.
it is the presence of conviction, despite our human emotions.
to feel suffering
and to still trust that God knows what He's doing,
even when we do not.
not to avoid or ignore our emotions and thoughts,
and pretend all is well,
but rather to still believe
when body, emotions, and thoughts are telling us absolutely everything otherwise,
that the soul knows the Truth of who God is.

open hands,
release control.

i cannot imagine who i would be
without the experience of Courteney
but in the strangest way,
i also cannot imagine who i would be now
without the experience of *losing* Courteney.

although it is still painful,
although breakdowns still happen frequently,
although there is an endless search
for similar traits in every person i meet,
looking at stranger's teeth, or how they laugh,
their hands, or how they speak.
i find her everywhere and in everyone.

yet i almost feel grateful (surprisingly so)
of the ways it has shaped me and who it has made me -

i never thought
i would feel *any* sort of gratitude
toward grief at all.

but God, if this is the kind of peace you provide –
i trust you.
i trust you.
i trust you.

and even when this peace isn't present –
i trust you.
i trust you.
i trust you.

i surrender.

HOME

i ache for the day
where my soul takes flight.

i feel the thirst.
what it means to be
h o m e s i c k.
my soul
restlessly knocking
on the door
of my ribcage,
aching to be released.
my essence
desiring to ascend,
attempting to rise,
wanting to let go
and soar with
open arms,
into the sky's ocean
that is
God's love.

i flirt with this world,
but it is not home.
my soul craves something
m o r e.

heaven may sound
like a dream -
        b u t
        heaven is
        so
        r e a l,
        so
        p a l p a b l e,
that earth
will actually feel like a dream.

this entire life of yours
will one day seem like a distant memory,
like someone else's biography that you had once read.
you will feel connected to your story,
but see it from the author's perspective,
finally understanding why

it all happened
the way it did.

the suffering
will feel distant,
almost insignificant,
compared to the
eternal weight of glory
waiting for us.

that is why i pray
you hold on through the night.
one which feels endless.
because soon,
the sun will rise
and you will remember
again
what it feels like to be awake.

the good & the bad,
the joy & the sorrow,
the pleasure & the pain.
all of it is t e m p o r a r y.
        and isn't that what makes it so beautiful?
            so monumental?
                to take in every // single // part.
inhale it.
hold it for as long as you can
and savor every second.

if you don't like what you are experiencing,
remember
seasons always change
and feelings always pass.

although this current season of life
is chaotic and hard,
God put you here
and that's enough
to remain.
everything that needs to happen
is.
the circumstances and events,
the people in your life.
God is even guiding
your interior life.

what you're thinking.
what you're feeling.
it is not wrong,
it is not too little
or too much,
and it is not happening
too late or too soon.

after enduring all of the waves,
the tides,
both high + low,
you did it.

> the ones you brutally fought through,
> using every ounce of strength and energy.
> flailing underwater,
> not knowing when you would get your next breath;

the ones you dove under
into the quiet break
to escape the chaos overhead;

> and the ones you let wash over you
> and carry you
> with open hands
> in whatever direction
> they so pleased;

you did it.
- you made it to the other side -
regardless of how you got here.

so for now,
float along
on your back,
letting the rhythm of the waves take you
and feeling the sun kiss your skin.

soon enough,
we will all float home.

the divine union.
the joyful celebration.
the homecoming.
to fully know
and to be fully known.

to be held
in an eternal embrace
of grandiose love.

i cannot wait
to finally meet my Maker
face to face
and to be welcomed home
with open arms,
first by God,
and then by Courteney.
the euphoric reunion
with my best friend.

where
death no longer reigns,
and grief no longer holds power.

not to spoil the ending,
but -
it is good.

Notes

Notes

About the Author

Katherine Flynn Plucinsky is an emerging author from Denver, Colorado whose debut, High Tides & Open Hands, chronicles her journey through grief. With a background in faith and spirituality, Plucinsky's work touches on themes of resiliency, healing, and the power of surrender. Her blend of poetry-prose is deeply honest and raw, inspiring readers to engage in their own stories. Follow her on Instagram at @katherineplu where she displays her affinity for sunrises, coffee shops, wine, and her deep love of the sea.

www.ingramcontent.com/pod-product-compliance
Lightning Source LLC
Chambersburg PA
CBHW030108240426
43661CB00031B/1332/J